Rocking Horse

Addressing the Problems of Carnality and Legality

By
Marty A. Cauley

© Copyright 2011
Second Edition
All rights reserved

Misthological Press
1231 Monteith Branch Road
Sylva, NC 28779

All rights reserved. No part of this book may be reproduced in any form without the prior written permission of the author, except as provided by USA copyright law.

For the author's online articles and for updates concerning his coming releases, see www.UnconditionalSecurity.org. The author's email address is: Misthologist@misthology.org.

"Unless otherwise noted, all Scripture quotations are taken from the New American Standard Bible®. Copyright © 1960, 1962, 1963, 1968, 1971, 1972, 1973, 1975, 1977, 1995 by The Lockman Foundation Used by permission." (www.Lockman.org)

Unless otherwise noted, the 1977 edition of New American Standard Bible is the edition used in the present book and abbreviated as the NAS.

All emphases in quoted material are added unless otherwise noted.

Books by the Author

1. *The Race of Grace*—introductory book in which performance related themes (such as perseverance) are considered essential for rewards in heaven. Entrance into heaven, in contrast, is regarded as free. A strong defense of unconditional security derived from believers being given to Jesus is a particular strength of this book.
2. *Is Heaven a Gift or a Reward?*—while some assert that heaven is a reward in some sense, this book maintains that regarding heaven itself as a gift is best.
3. *Breaking the Rocking Horse*—introductory book regarding the distinction between having eternal life as a gift versus obtaining it as a reward. An overview of the outer darkness and an exegetical treatment of the parable of the soils are this book's primary strengths.
4. *Mere Christianity and Moral Christianity*—a more comprehensive discussion regarding perseverance (and other performance related themes) as being needed for rewards in heaven rather than for entrance into heaven. This book provides both introductory material and advanced treatments.
5. *Woolly Wolves and Woolless Sheep*—a rejection of the notion that profession of salvation is proven genuine by the way a person lives. This book focuses on the parable of the sheep and the goats and shows the inadequacy of conditional security in interpreting this parable.
6. *Sheep and Goats*—an advanced discussion of the parable of the sheep and goats that evaluates four interpretations that are compatible with unconditional security.
7. *Sealed and Secure*—a thorough defense of a popular argument for unconditional security that also defends the premise of unconditional promises.
8. *Fallen from Grace but Not from Perfection*—an advanced defense of unconditional security which affirms that believers can fall from grace but not fall from perfection.
9. *Salvation*—a study of how the verb *save* and the noun *salvation* are used in the NT. A comprehensive chart of NT usage is provided.
10. *Believe*—an aspectual defense of unconditional security that examines how the verb *believe* is used in the Gospel of John. A comprehensive chart of metaphors for *believe* in the Gospel of John is provided also.
11. *Carnal Corinth*—an affirmation of the categorical existence of carnal Christians within the Corinthian epistles.
12. *The Outer Darkness*—a *magnum opus* that ties together the author's arguments for unconditional security and conditional rewards.

See UnconditionalSecurity.org for the release status of these books.

Table of Contents

TABLE OF CONTENTS I
TRANSLATIONS IV
CITATIONS IV
ABBREVIATIONS IV
TABLE OF ILLUSTRATIONS V
ACKNOWLEDGMENTS VII
TECHNICAL TERMS VIII

CHAPTER 1. THE NATURE OF THE PROBLEM 1
INCONSISTENCY 1
LOGIC 3
WITHOUT COST 5
COSTLY 6
SOLUTION 8

CHAPTER 2. THE NATURE OF REWARDS 11
POSITIVE REWARDS 11
NEGATIVE REWARDS 11
LICENTIOUSNESS AND LEGALISM 12
OUTER DARKNESS 14
    When 14
    Text 16
    Who 17
        Believers Need to Stay Alert 17
        Believers Addressed by Warning 18
        Believers Today Do Not Know That Day 19
        Believers Are His Own 19
        Believers Are Called Slaves 19
        Believers Are Entrusted 20
        Believers Can Hide Their Gifts and Nature 23
        Believers Judged at This Time 25
        Believers Have Identical Relationships 27
        Believers Have Received What Was Offered 29
        Believers' Status Not Forfeitable at This Time 30
        Believers Can Suffer Loss 30
        Believers Can Be Cast Out 31
        Believers Are in the Outer Darkness 32
        Believers May Weep and Gnash Their Teeth 32
    Summary 33

CHAPTER 3. THE NATURE OF THE SPIRIT'S FRUIT 35

ROOT DETERMINES FRUIT 35
FRUIT OF THE SPIRIT 35
ROOT-FRUIT RHETORIC 38
REAP WHAT YOU SOW 41
THE NATURE OF THE INHERITANCE 42

CHAPTER 4. THE NATURE OF THE BELIEVER'S FRUIT 45

INHERENT MERIT 45
ADD WORKS 46
DO YOUR BEST 49
ACTIVITY NOT PASSIVITY 50
FORMER SINS 52
ABIDE IN ME 53

CHAPTER 5. THE NATURE OF THE SOIL 55

SOIL DETERMINES FRUIT 55
HARD SOIL 56
ROCKY SOIL 57
    Implanted 57
    Fall Away 59
    Believe and Be Saved 59
    Tares 62
    Immature Roots 62
THORNY SOIL 64
    Mature Roots 65
    Immature Fruits 66
GOOD SOIL 66
    Perseverance 67
    Honest, Good, and Loyal 67

CHAPTER 6. THE NATURE OF PROVEITIST EVIDENCE 73

JUST BECAUSE 73
NECESSARY FRUITS 75
CONDITIONAL FRUITS 80
    Singular Fruit of the Spirit 81
    Singular Fruit of Faith 81

CHAPTER 7. THE NATURE OF JUSTIFICATION BY FAITH 85

PHARISEE AND PUBLICAN 85
MANIFESTATIVE RIGHTEOUSNESS 89
PROVE IT 92
MERCY 94

CHAPTER 8. THE NATURE OF QUALITY VERSUS QUANTITY 97

HOW MUCH FRUIT 97
JESUS' DEATH 98

SPIRITUAL SUICIDE	101
CONFIRMATION OF CONDITIONALISM	103

CHAPTER 9. THE NATURE OF PERSEVERANCE 105

PERSEVERE YOUR WAY TO HEAVEN	105
KINGSHIP	105
REWARD OF RULERSHIP	105

CHAPTER 10. THE NATURE OF THE DANGER 111

IMPLICIT IS STILL DEADLY	111
BELIEVING THAT YOU BELIEVE	114
CONTROL OF YOUR LIFE	116

APPENDIX 1. JUDGMENT IS ALWAYS BASED ON WORKS 121

JUDGED FOR WORKS	121
JUDGED BY WORKS	122
JUDGED ON THE BASIS OF WORKS	122
FALSE DICHOTOMY	122
JUDGED FROM THE BOOK OF WORKS	122

APPENDIX 2. ENOCHIAN DARKNESS 125

ENDNOTES 129

INDEXES 144

Greek Index	144
Subject Index	144
Extrabiblical Index	149
Scripture Index	150

Translations

BBE	English Bible in Basic English
CJB	Complete Jewish Bible
CSB	Holman Christian Standard Bible
ESV	English Standard Version
GWN	God's Word to the Nations Version
KJV	King James Version
MRD	James Murdock Translation
NAB	New American Bible [Roman Catholic translation]
NAS	New American Standard Translation (1977 edition)
NET	New English Translation
NIV	New International Version
NKJ	New King James Version
NLT	New Living Translation
NRS	New Revised Standard Version of the Bible
NTME	New Testament in Modern English
RSV	Revised Standard Version
RWB	Revised Webster Update
TM	Translation Mine
WEB	English Noah Webster Bible

Citations

BDAG	*A Greek-English Lexicon of the New Testament and Other Early Christian Literature*, ed. Frederick W. Danker, 3rd ed. Chicago: University of Chicago Press, 2000. Via BibleWorks.
GNTC	*The Grace New Testament Commentary*, ed. Robert N. Wilkin. Denton, TX: Grace Evangelical Society, 2010.
L-N	*Louw-Nida Greek-English Lexicon of the New Testament Based on Semantic Domains*, 2nd ed., eds. J. P. Louw and E. A. Nida, 1988. Via BibleWorks.

Abbreviations

Bema	The Greek word for judgment is *bema* and popularly is used as an abbreviated term for *Judgment Seat of Christ* (where Christians are judged after the rapture). It pertains to rewards in heaven.
GES	*Grace Evangelical Society*
OSAS	*Once Saved Always Saved*

Table of Illustrations

Illustration 1. The Heavenly Rocking Horse 1
Illustration 2. Typical Pastor's Offer of the Free Gift 2
Illustration 3. Costly-Free Heaven 6
Illustration 4. Costly-Free Gospel 7
Illustration 5. The Broken Free-Costly Horse 7
Illustration 6. Simple Solution 8
Illustration 7. Purely-Free Preacher 9
Illustration 8. Duality of Eternal Life 9
Illustration 9. Rewards Are According to Works 12
Illustration 10. Only Two Costly-Free Landing Strips 13
Illustration 11. Bema Judgment of Believers 15
Illustration 12. Some Christians Hide It 24
Illustration 13. Some Christians Shine It 25
Illustration 14. Distinction in Judgments 26
Illustration 15. The Unworthy Slave of Mt 25:13-30 33
Illustration 16. Lost or Saved? 35
Illustration 17. Lost or Spiritual or What? 36
Illustration 18. Carnal Overlapping 36
Illustration 19. The Fruity Rocking Horse 37
Illustration 20. The Broken Lost-Spiritual Horse 37
Illustration 21. Root-Fruit Canoe 39
Illustration 22. Entrance Versus Inheritance 43
Illustration 23. Free Entrance and Free Inheritance 43
Illustration 24. Free Entrance but Costly Inheritance 44
Illustration 25. Add/Supply Works to Your Faith 46
Illustration 26. Faith + Works 47
Illustration 27. Works as Evidence of Faith 47
Illustration 28. Additions to Faith 48
Illustration 29. Passive Paddling 50
Illustration 30. Tragic Ending 51
Illustration 31. The Parable of the Soils (Lk 8:4-15) 55
Illustration 32. Duality of Faith 60
Illustration 33. Problem Progression 65
Illustration 34. Root and Fruits 66
Illustration 35. The Active-Passive Rocking Horse 67
Illustration 36. The Broken Active-Passive Horse 68
Illustration 37. Very-Costly Preacher 68
Illustration 38. Four Soils, Three Roots, Two Fruits, One Perseverance 69
Illustration 39. Carnal Security is Germinating Security 71
Illustration 40. Just Because 74
Illustration 41. Prove It! 75
Illustration 42. No Fruits…Then No Root! 76
Illustration 43. Fruit Determines Destiny 77

Illustration 44. Crisscross of Tree and Fruit 78
Illustration 45. Just Because of the Root 78
Illustration 46. Bear or Burn 79
Illustration 47. Performance Baseball 80
Illustration 48. Broken Faith 81
Illustration 49. Apple of Saving Faith 82
Illustration 50. Apple of Non-Saving Faith 82
Illustration 51. God-Enabled Performance for Heaven 86
Illustration 52. Saving-Enabling Grace 87
Illustration 53. Saving Grace-Works 87
Illustration 54. Flat-Tire Believers 89
Illustration 55. Prove You are a Disciple 91
Illustration 56. Costly-Free Mercy 94
Illustration 57. Quality and Quantity 97
Illustration 58. Did Jesus Lose Eternal Life? 98
Illustration 59. Uphill Costly-Free Fight to Heaven 101
Illustration 60. Costly-Free Perseverance 106
Illustration 61. Is Perseverance Necessary? 107
Illustration 62. Broken Costly-Free Perseverance 107
Illustration 63. Pick One and Only One 108
Illustration 64. Cross-Eyed Gift and Crown 109
Illustration 65. Sanctified Common Sense 110
Illustration 66. I believe—But Not Really 111
Illustration 67. I Am Saved If… 112
Illustration 68. It is Finished If… 113
Illustration 69. Mistaken Belief 114
Illustration 70. Hard to Enter 115
Illustration 71. Three Types of People 118
Illustration 72. Two Sets of Books 123
Illustration 73. Darkness Outside the King's Palace 126
Illustration 74. The Darkness Outside is Inside the Gates of Paradise 128
Illustration 75. Positive Progression 136
Illustration 76. I Believe that I Believe 138
Illustration 77. Mathematical Problems and Answers 139
Illustration 78. Soteriological Problems and Answers 140

Acknowledgments

To my mother, Gladys J. Cauley, and brother, Philip Cauley, I would like to express thanks for proofreading the larger manuscript of *Mere Christianity and Moral Christianity*. They suggested that I write a short work that would summarize my key points without going into technical detail. My sons have also made a similar suggestion. The present book represents my attempt to do so. At the same time, I included an abridged chapter from my much larger book, *The Outer Darkness*, and introduced some related concepts found in that work. Therefore, the present book serves as an introduction to the much fuller discussions found elsewhere in my writings. For technical defenses, integration, and citations pertaining to the positions introduced herein, please see the larger works.

As to this shorter work, my mother, brother, and sons have read it. And I am thankful for their contributions. Trent Hilderbrand (a friend from the GES Webboard) has assisted in proofreading, as has Scott Crawford (who has been a constant source of encouragement). Over the many years that I have been working on *The Outer Darkness*, Lewis Schoettle has provided guidance and inspiration. As that writing project grew to span many years and hundreds of pages, he made the original inquiry as to the possibility of my producing a summary work. Despite my initial hesitation, I have conceded by providing the present book, which he was gracious enough to proofread as well.

Technical Terms

Costly-free advocate: someone who believes that entrance into heaven is both costly and free for the believer.

Prove-it advocate: a costly-free advocate who believes that fruit is necessary proof of salvation: *If you do not have this fruit, then you were never saved initially.* Perseverance is necessary to prove that you are saved and to enter heaven.

Proveitist: an advocate of prove-it theology.

Lose-it advocate: a costly-free advocate who believes that those who do not persevere lose the gift of eternal life.

Forfeitist: an advocate of lose-it theology.

Conditional security: the belief that perseverance is necessary to enter heaven. (Prove-it and lose-it theologies both advocate conditional security).

Conditional securitist: someone who believes that perseverance is necessary to enter heaven.

Conditionalist: a term for *conditional securitist*.

Unconditional security: the belief that entrance into heaven does not require perseverance.

Unconditional securitist: someone who believes that perseverance is not necessary to enter heaven.

Securitist: (a term for *unconditional securitist*): an advocate of keep-it theology.

Keep-it advocate: a purely-free advocate who believes that perseverance is not necessary to keep the free gift of eternal life. (Keep-it theology advocates unconditional security.)

Chapter 1.
The Nature of the Problem

Inconsistency

Many discussions of heaven within Christendom rock back-and-forth between presenting heaven as being a free yet costly gift. Somehow this free gift is supposed to be costly to the intended recipient. Assumptions rather than explanations seem to abound in such presentations as to how heaven can be both free and costly. Contradictory statements are made back-and-forth within the course of most sermons. Such seesawing statements typically are not made back-to-back so that the incompatibility of such rocking is not so glaring in calling heaven both free and costly. Still, the rational mind (that has not been lulled to sleep by the hypnotic swaying back-and-forth) cries out for elucidation, not mere assertion.

Illustration 1. The Heavenly Rocking Horse

Over the years, churchgoers simply grow accustomed to such inconsistencies. If a pastor is preaching that salvation is a free gift, one can almost rest assured that within the course of the sermon, he will make at least one statement that attaches a price tag to this repeatedly free offer. If the unexpected happens and the pastor does not discount his belief in the freeness of the offer during the course of some particular sermon, he almost certainly will do so when he reaches the invitation. He will add at least one or more stipulations that, to the thinking person, would raise a question about the actual freeness of the offer.

Illustration 2. Typical Pastor's Offer of the Free Gift

How many times have you heard pastors call for repentance and commitment as conditions for receiving or keeping the free gift of eternal life? By stressing that the free gift of eternal life is free while simultaneously or subsequently denying that it truly is free, they speak contradictory statements. Calling for (1) repentance from sin, (2) commitment of life, and (3) perseverance in such commitments are performance issues that certainly are appropriate in the context of discipleship. Making such performance themes necessary to enter heaven, however, even while simultaneously preaching that heaven is free, necessarily smacks of inconsistency. Heaven ends up being conditioned on threefold performance: (1) repentance of old behavior; (2) commitment to new behavior; and (3) perseverance in bearing good fruit in terms of new behavior. The real meaning of such pastoral appeals comes through crystal clear when expressed in terms of their logical implications:

- Commit your *performance* to Christ.
- Surrender your *performance* to Christ.
- Give your *performance* to Christ.
- Trusting Christ with your *performance* is the way you trust Christ for eternal life.

Needless to say, eternal life clearly is not a free gift when presented with the full ramifications of such invitations. In the above illustration, a fictional picture of the typical pastor is used to represent these offsetting appeals. Over the years, I could have placed many faces in that circle. Perhaps, you may recognize the face of your pastor belonging in this circle as well. If you are a pastor reading this book, perhaps your own face belongs within it, perhaps not. Genuine exceptions exist, but they are exceedingly rare.

Logic

Is expecting logical consistency within sermons wrong? Is it wrong to approach the Bible rationally? Of course not. Quite the contrary, the Bible enjoins us to be logical. Being created in the image of God means, among other things, that we were created as rational beings because God is a rational being. Logic is rooted in the nature of God and thus in our nature. At our deepest level, we do not appreciate contradictions or doubletalk. We have an innate desire for truth—for logical consistency. Sure, there are limits to what logic can do. Scripture takes precedence over logic. Logic is a servant to Scripture. Even so, it is a disservice to Scripture to dispense with the service performed by logic.

The very word *theology* is derived from the combination of two biblical Greek words: *theos* (*God*) and *logos* (*logic*). Biblical theology is logical teaching about God. Sermons that are true to the nature of God will not violate God's moral laws or His logical laws. The axiomatic *law of non-contradiction* (A is not non-A) is that no two contradictory statements can be true at the same time and in the same sense. Not even God can do what is logically impossible, such as making a round square, because that would go against His very nature. Granted, mysteries exist that go *beyond* human reason, but they do not go *against* it. The human *inability* to know truth comprehensively does not nullify the ability to know truth *fundamentally*. God is truth, and truth is the means to knowing God. Jesus identified Himself as truth and the means to the Father (Jn 14:6). Since we can know truth, we can know God fundamentally.

Just as A cannot be non-A, just as light is not darkness, just as sweet is not bitter, just as it is wrong to "call evil good, and good evil" (Is 5:20), so it is wrong to call *free costly*! Pastors are being irrational when they talk of the free gift of eternal life as being costly to the believer. The gift is costly to the Giver (God), of course, but it is free to the recipient (the believer). The Bible tells us "to refute those who contradict" sound doctrine (Tit 1:9). How can contradictions to sound doctrine be refuted if sound doctrine is composed of contractions? Obviously, sound doctrine is presumed to be free of contradictions. Any pastoral supposition that sound doctrine has contradictions is antithetical to sound doctrine.

According to Rom 12:1, Christians are supposed to be *rational* (*logikos*) in their worship of God. Most translations render this word as *spiritual* or *reasonable*. If the requested worship is in accord with reason, it is rational and *reasonable*. As to the rendering of *spiritual*, certainly this type of worship feeds our spirit (the metaphysical as opposed to physical dimension of our being). Still, the word in question is *logikos* (*logical*), the adjective form of *logos* (*logic*). Why not simply translate the verse (as some translations do) as referring to an act of worship that is *logical*? This verse is exhorting Christians to present their bodies as a living and holy sacrifice, acceptable to God, which is their "logical service of worship" (TM).

Christians are supposed to be logicians, at least to a reasonable degree. They are expected to offer themselves as living sacrifices to God because doing so is logical, not mechanical or external. In the OT, no appeal was made to the intelligence of the sacrificial offering. You did not try to persuade your lamb as to the logical reasonableness of why it should hop up on the altar and be slain. Lambs could not offer themselves of their own free, intelligent, informed decision. Animals are said to be illogical.[*] Human beings, on the other hand, are given free choice and allowed to make an informed decision. God gives this invitation: "'Come now, and let us reason together,' says the Lord, 'Though your sins are as scarlet, they will be as white as snow; though they are red like crimson, they will be like wool'" (Is 1:18). God expects humans to reason with Him because He is reasonable.

To be sure, God's thoughts are higher than our thoughts (Is 55:8-9). Calculus is a higher branch of mathematics than arithmetic. Yet this does not mean that calculus is irrational or contradictory to arithmetic. In the same way, this biblical text from Isaiah should not be used as a proof text to assert that God is unknowable, irrational, or illogical. God is not an animal; neither are we animals in comparison to God. We were created in the image of God and retain the image of God sufficiently to reason with God. To be sure, God's logic is higher than ours in *degree*. However, in terms of *fundamental nature*, we have the foundation by which to know God by means of sound thinking. In this very context from Isaiah, God clearly asserts that He may be found by those who seek Him (Is 55:6-7). Since God is truth, we are to seek Him who is truth through the avenue of truth—noncontradictory thinking. Therefore, when a pastor is preaching something that is logically contradictory to sound thinking, he is teaching something that is contrary to sound doctrine.

---

[*] The Bible refers to animals as unreasoning (2Pet 2:12; Jude 1:10). The Greek word used here is *alogos* (the negation of *logos*) and refers to being *irrational, unreasonable, illogical*. In these two passages, the Scripture is rebuking people who speak illogically in speaking evil. People should not live like animals nor should preachers preach like animals.

Christians are commanded to examine the gospel presented by preachers to see if what they are preaching is contrary to the biblical message: "But even though we, or an angel from heaven, should preach to you a gospel contrary to that which we have preached to you, let him be accursed. As we have said before, so I say again now, if any man is preaching to you a gospel contrary to that which you received, let him be accursed" (Gal 1:8-9). A false message and false messenger must be denounced. To do otherwise would be unchristian.

Without Cost

The OT invitation to salvation is: "Ho! Every one who thirsts, come to the waters....without money and without cost" (Is 55:1).* Jesus picks up this theme in the NT and speaks of living water as a gift (Jn 4:10). In the closing book of the NT, Jesus promises: "I will give to the one who thirsts from the spring of the water of life without cost" (Rev 21:6). The closing invitation of the Bible is: "Let the one who is thirsty come; let the one who wishes take the water of life without cost" (Rev 22:17).

Pastors who try to barter the water of life for control of one's life are not doing the Lord any favors. They are poisoning the water of life with works-righteousness.† The Lord insists that the water of life be taken purely and freely. Those trying to earn the water of life are contaminating its freeness. The alternative to taking the water of life freely is deadly.

The Bible is insistent that the justification (i.e., righteousness) necessary to enter heaven must be "apart from works" (Rom 3:28).‡ This righteousness is only offered "apart from works" (Rom 4:6). It must be received as a "free gift" (Rom 5:15-16). Entrance into heaven cannot be obtained by performance. One cannot compromise this entrance by considering this free offer costly. These texts are very well known. So why do preachers try to barter the water of life for control of one's life?

---

* Like the water of life, eternal life is offered as a "free gift" (Rom 6:23).

† **Works-righteousness** is a derogatory label applied to the teaching which asserts that we are saved from hell on the basis of "works of righteousness which we have done." Such a teaching rejects the clear biblical summation that teaches that we are not saved from hell on the basis of "works of righteousness which we have done" (Tit 3:5). Biblically, by faith, we must rest our justification pertaining to getting to heaven on the **imputational/legal** righteousness of Christ *apart from* any of our works (Rom 3:28; 4:6). Those trusting in **impartational/practical** righteousness in order to reach heaven are trusting wrongly in works-righteousness for a benefit it was never intended to bestow.

‡ Conditionalism rejects final salvation (i.e., salvation from hell) by *faith apart from works* because *faith needs works* to be saving according to conditionalists.

Costly

The Lord exhorts those contemplating becoming His disciples to count the cost. Discipleship is costly business. Such discipleship requires you to take up your cross, even to the point of giving up your possessions (Lk 14:26-33). Emphatically, this level of commitment requires that you take up your cross daily (Lk 9:23). Daily, wholehearted performance is required to meet such uncompromising demands. Astoundingly, the majority of pastors preach as if the Bible were calling for this discipleship as the means to enter heaven as a free gift. The bizarre result is that heaven is pictured as a free gift that costs you everything. Tragically, this false gospel leads to hell rather than to heaven. The Lord will not sell heaven, even though costly-free preachers present Him as doing so.

Illustration 3. Costly-Free Heaven

Those preachers who portray heaven as a free gift that costs you everything are presenting an oxymoronic gospel that attacks the character of our Lord, practically picturing Him as selling costly-free tickets to heaven. Such a gospel depicts Jesus as a shady character who blurs the distinction between free and costly (or as a moron who cannot tell the difference between free and costly). This costly-free gospel is not a saving gospel but a demonic imitation instead. Our Lord does not speak with a forked tongue. Nevertheless, many pastors, supposedly speaking as His representatives, certainly do. Perhaps such pastors technically are not lying because they truly may believe that they are telling the truth (while being blinded to the truth). Nevertheless, since they are presenting a lie, the charge of speaking with a forked tongue sticks. Certainly, many such pastors are preaching the gospel with all sincerity. Even so, sincerity is no substitute for accuracy. As the old adage goes, one can be sincere yet be sincerely wrong.

Chapter 1. The Nature of the Problem

Illustration 4. Costly-Free Gospel

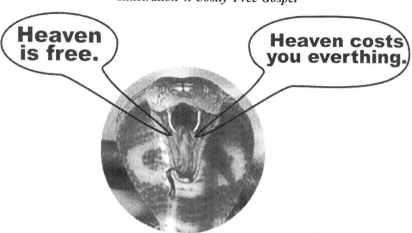

In many pulpits, getting to heaven is made contingent on behavior. All the while, such pastors stress that salvation is not conditioned on the way one lives. Such inconsistency is not a travesty but a tragedy. As well-intentioned as they may be, pastors who teach a performance-based salvation from hell actually are teaching a poisoned gospel that leads to hell. These pseudo preachers attach their fine print to their correct statements regarding freeness so that the freeness of the gospel is actually removed. Even in the best cases, conditional security—a security conditioned on performance—ends up being implicitly affirmed in such cases.

Illustration 5. The Broken Free-Costly Horse

The only way to break free of this deception is to break the myth of the costly-free rocking horse. Logically, this horse is unable to sustain the weight placed upon it by costly-free pastors.

Solution

The solution to this unnecessary costly-free dilemma is very simple: Recognize that certain aspects of heaven are free; other aspects are costly. Entrance into heaven is offered freely. Rewards in heaven are costly.

Illustration 6. Simple Solution

Just as there are some things that parents may give to their children freely as presents, so there are some things that God gives to His children freely just because they are His children. On the other hand, loving parents may give certain things as rewards to their children for good behavior or for performing certain tasks. God also rewards His children in like fashion. Specifically, the crown of life is promised to God's children who are loving and faithful (Jam 1:12; Rev 2:10).

God rewards godly character and performance. Obviously, a crown conditioned on Christian virtues is not given freely. Therefore, one form of eternal life (namely the water of life) is free, but another form of eternal life (namely the crown of life) is costly. The Bible is not speaking contradictorily when it speaks of two different aspects of eternal life—one being free and the other being costly. The *law of non-contradiction* (A is not non-A) is not being violated because eternal life is being spoken of in two different senses.

Likewise, as noted above, righteousness may be given freely as a gift. On the other hand, righteousness additionally may be achieved as a reward for loving the Lord in terms of fighting the good fight, finishing the course, and keeping the faith (2Tim 4:7-8). Lovingly persevering is rewarded by the Lord with a crown.

Chapter 1. The Nature of the Problem

Illustration 7. Purely-Free Preacher

In counterpoint to costly-free advocates, the purely-free proponent makes a sharp and consistent contrast between the freeness of the gift and the costliness of rewards. Even when a purely-free speaker makes back-to-back statements about the free nature of the gift of life and the costly nature of the crown of life, he is not mouthing a contradiction or speaking out of both sides of his mouth. Instead, he is being straightforward about the contrasting, yet complementary, dimensions of eternal life.

Illustration 8. Duality of Eternal Life

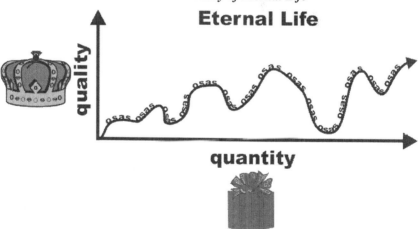

Quantitatively, the gift of eternal life goes on freely forever. This aspect of eternal life is popularly referred to as OSAS (*Once Saved Always Saved*). Unconditional security is a more technically precise label. Even some costly-free pastors will affirm OSAS, but they do not believe it is unconditional since they believe that perseverance is necessary to reach heaven. Purely-free pastors, on the other hand, acknowledge that the gift of eternal life is not conditioned on perseverance in the faith. Instead, they maintain that perseverance is necessary for the crown of life—a superlative, qualitative experience of the eternal life already possessed as a gift. In other words, all believers will live in heaven, but not all believers will live as rulers in heaven. Rulership with Christ is conditioned on the believer enduring (i.e., persevering) to the end of his or her life (2Tim 2:12a). Those believers who do not endure will be denied positions of rulership with Christ (2Tim 2:12b). This fuller dimension of eternal life is popularly called abundant life in deference to the Lord's distinction: "I came that they might have [eternal] life, and might have it abundantly" (Jn 10:10). Eternal life can be had and experienced at various degrees.

Chapter 2.
The Nature of Rewards

Positive Rewards

Despite the biblical stress on rewards, many costly-free preachers will speak in a deriding manner of rewards, seemingly presenting themselves as more Christian than Christ. Since they look down their noses at those who promote rewards, logically they would have to look down on Christ as teaching an inferior brand of Christianity to their supposedly more spiritual approach that shuns rewards as being an inferior means of motivation. Because their theology makes getting to heaven a reward, they have little room in their theology for truly meaningful distinctions within heaven regarding rewards. Even so, some within their own theological camp will try at least to pay homage to the obvious biblical emphasis on positive rewards.

Negative Rewards

Costly-free pastors face an almost insurmountable task in affirming the biblical doctrine of negative rewards. Indeed, very few of them scale such heights. The vast majority of such interpreters prefer to ride their rocking horse in the lowlands. A much better mount is required to ride up to the mountain peaks regarding negative rewards. The problem for most preachers scaling these heights is not attributable to lack of clarity within the biblical record, however. The Bible says that God will reward everyone (lost and saved) according to their works (Rev 22:12).[*] Everyone includes believers. Christians are a subset of those who are to be judged and rewarded. As believers, Christians will never come into judgment where the issue is life versus death in terms of heaven versus hell (Jn 5:24). Nevertheless, even believers will be judged in terms of rewards. The Bible is very clear that the judgment that applies to everyone applies to Christian brethren as well:

> [10]But you, why do you judge your brother? Or you again, why do you regard your brother with contempt? For we will all stand before the judgment seat of God. [11]For it is written, "As I live,

---

[*] The lost are rewarded in hell. Believers are rewarded in heaven. Nevertheless, not all rewards dispensed in heaven are good in the sense of being enjoyable. Christians will be rewarded for the bad they have done. Such rewards will not be positive.

says the Lord, every knee will bow to Me, and every tongue will confess to God." [12]So then each one of us will give an account of himself to God. (Rom 14:10-12; TM)

Everyone will be judged according to their works. This everyone includes Christians as is made clear by the biblical record in the above text.

Illustration 9. Rewards Are According to Works

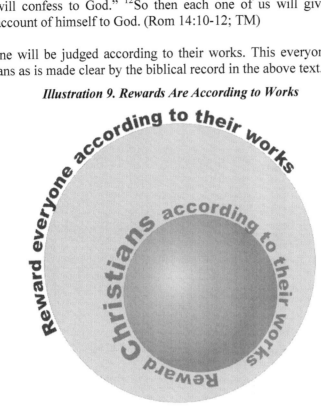

Not all rewards are positive. Speaking yet again to Christians, the Bible distinctly teaches, "For we must all appear before the *judgment seat* [*bema*] of Christ, that each one may be recompensed for his deeds in the body, according to what he has done, **whether good or bad**" (2Cor 5:10). God is not going to reward the bad that a Christian has done with positive rewards. Even Christians will be repaid negatively for the wrongs they have done (Col 3:25). Disobedient believers will be repaid with negative rewards for negative behavior.

Licentiousness and Legalism

Many costly-free preachers falsely accuse consistent purely-free apologists with preaching licentiousness. From the costly-free perspective, since heaven costs you everything, you have already paid a very dear price just to make it to heaven. Because you have already given everything you have just to enter heaven, you really have nothing else to contribute toward earning any special rewards in heaven. All that really matters in their costly-free theology is reaching heaven. So if you preach that heaven is purely-free, then, from the costly-free perspective, you are teaching that the way a person lives ultimately does not really matter. The costly-free preachers will regard a purely-free presentation of heaven as teaching licentiousness and object that a person cannot live like the devil and still make it to heaven.[1]

Illustration 10. Only Two Costly-Free Landing Strips

The costly-free aversion to acknowledging the impact of negative rewards causes costly-free advocates to land in legalism.[2] That is not a landing strip that anyone—lost or saved—should take. One prevailing reason that costly-free preachers wind up in legalism is because they have nowhere to land a believer who is clearly marked by carnal behavior—other than as ruling in heaven or suffering in hell. Naturally, legalists opt for the latter option. An intermediate possibility that provides another landing strip for the carnal believer would have given the costly-free position somewhere to land other than legalism. This intermediate position is found in a strong affirmation of negative biblical rewards. Carnal believers are not going to get off entirely free for living licentiously.

An affirmation of negative rewards for carnal believers is not only necessary biblically, it is healthy theologically. It is a strong deterrent to legalism and licentiousness. Those who deny the negative aspects of rewards only have two landing strips on which the licentious believer can land—suffering in hell or ruling in heaven. Another landing strip exists, however, that enables one to avoid legalism.

Outer Darkness

The most picturesque portrayal of rewards for believers comes in Mt 25:14-30. In this parable, two out of three slaves serve the Lord well and are rewarded with hearing Him say, "Well done" (Mt 25:21-23). The desire to hear those two words is the heart's desire of every sensible Christian. The details of the parable concerning the third slave likewise make it necessary for any reasonable believer to conclude that the alternative experience—that of being cast into *the outer darkness*—represents a very real possibility for licentious or lazy believers and thus pertains to the loss of heavenly rewards.

When

In order to better understand the context of this parable, a rudimentary understanding of the time frame being discussed within it is necessary. This parable is part of a teaching that Jesus gave privately to four of His disciples on Mount Olivet in response to their questions: "As He was sitting on the Mount of Olives opposite the temple, Peter and James and John and Andrew were questioning Him privately" (Mk 13:3; cp. Mt 24:3). Therefore, those being addressed in these parables by the word *you* refers to these four genuine believers and thus signifies that the intended application is for genuine believers. This discourse fittingly is called the Mount Olivet Discourse.

Not only must this parable be studied within the context of this discourse, it must be interpreted in the broader context of biblical prophecy. A fundamental grasp of prophecy will be very helpful in determining what event the Lord is portraying. The Olivet Discourse discusses the tribulation. Understanding where this event occurs on the prophetic map is most useful. The tribulation will last seven years. For those who hold this view of the end of time (and thus believe that the rapture can happen at any time), the time indicator supplied by the Lord should be decisive. That the parable of the talents deals with the current church age (which takes place before the tribulation) is indicated in the very opening verse where Jesus says that we do not know when He will return. To illustrate this principle, Jesus uses this parable about servants who do not know when their master will return. This time frame cannot be referring to those living during the tribulation. (Those serving the Lord during the tribulation will be able to calculate the time of His return to the very day.) The passage is dealing with the unknown time of His return in the rapture.

The Lord confirms this understanding in Mt 25:19. The master is gone for a *long time* but may come back anytime. His coming is imminent but not immediate. This description only fits the rapture. The Lord is laying the foundation for the NT teaching of rapture. There is no sign anywhere in the parable to indicate the master's return. Because the passage is dealing with the rapture, it must be representing the *bema* judgment of genuine believers. The fact that the passage is contrasting what happens to faithful and unfaithful believers is indicated in numerous details.

Illustration 11. Bema Judgment of Believers

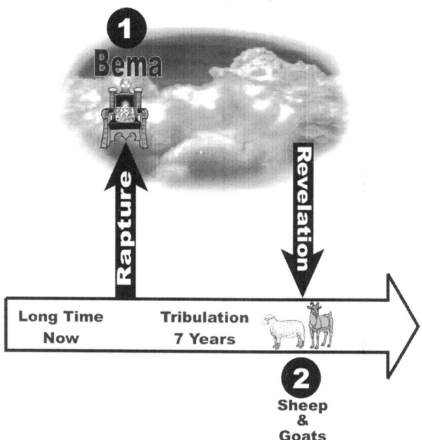

Within this series of parables, Jesus will refer to two different aspects of His return. ❶ The initial phase of His return happens at an unknown time: "Therefore be on the alert, for you do not know which day your Lord is coming" (Mt 24:42). Not only is the timing of this first phase unknown, it occurs at a time when not even believers (addressed by *you*) will expect it: "The Son of Man is coming at an hour when you do not think He will" (Mt 24:44). The Olivet parable regarding the outer darkness pertains to this phase. The Bible describes this phase of the Lord's return as the catching up into the clouds of believers who are then living on the earth to meet the Lord in the air: "Then we who are alive and remain shall be caught up together with them in the clouds to meet the Lord in the air, and thus we shall always be with the Lord" (1Thess 4:17). This transition is popularly called the *rapture* based on the Latin term for being caught up.

❷ The second phase of the Lord's return will occur at the end of the Great Tribulation (Mt 24:9-14). The number of those days have already been prophetically *shortened* (Mt 24:22) to precisely seven years by the OT (Dan 9:24-27). Specifically, the Lord will return 2,520 days[*] after the ratification of the peace treaty with Israel. The second half of this period is called the Great Tribulation. The peace treaty will be broken half way through the seven-year tribulation and commences this Great Tribulation. The second half of this tribulation also is specified within Scripture as 1,260[†] days (i.e., 2520/2). Believers living in that time period will not only be expecting the Lord to return at the end of the seven years, they will be able to mark the exact day of His return on their calendars. This phase refers to the revelation of Christ (Lk 17:30; 2Thess 1:7) when He returns all the way to earth in flaming fire and sets His foot down on the Mount of Olives. The mountain will split in two as a result (Zech 14:4). The Olivet parable regarding the judgment of the sheep and goats pertains to this phase.

Text

[13]Be on the **alert** then, for **you** do **not know the day nor the hour**. [14]For it is just like a man about to go on a journey, who called **his own slaves**, and **entrusted** his possessions to them. [15]And to one he gave five talents, to another, two, and to another, one, each according to his own ability; and he went on his journey. [16]Immediately the one who had received the five talents went and traded with them, and gained five more talents. [17]In the same manner the one who had received the two talents gained two more. [18]But he who received the one talent went away and dug in the ground, and **hid** his master's money. [19]Now after a **long time** the master of those slaves came and settled accounts with them. [20]And the one who had received the five talents came up and brought five more talents, saying, "**Master**, you entrusted five talents to me; see, I have gained five more talents." [21]His master said to him, "Well done, good and faithful slave; you were faithful with a few things, I will put you in charge of many things, enter into the joy of your master." [22]The one also who had received the two talents came up and said, "Master, you entrusted to me two talents; see, I have gained two more talents." [23]His master said to him, "Well done, good and faithful slave; you were faithful with a few

---

[*] A prophetic year would be 360 days, so 7 x 360 = 2,520.
[†] See Rev 11:3; 12:6.

things, I will put you in charge of many things; enter into the joy of your master." ²⁴And the one also who had **received** the one talent came up and said, "Master, I knew you to be a hard man, reaping where you did not sow, and gathering where you scattered no seed. ²⁵ "And I was afraid, and went away and hid your talent in the ground; see, you have what is yours." ²⁶But his master answered and said to him, "You wicked, lazy slave, you knew that I reap where I did not sow, and gather where I scattered no seed. ²⁷"Then you ought to have put my money in the bank, and on **my arrival** I would have received my money back with interest. ²⁸"Therefore **take away** the talent from him, and give it to the one who has the ten talents." ²⁹For to everyone who has shall more be given, and he shall have an abundance; but from the one who does not have, even what he does have shall be taken away. ³⁰And **cast out** the worthless slave into the **outer darkness**; in that place there shall be **weeping and gnashing of teeth**. (Mt 25:13-30)

Who

Believers Need to Stay Alert

First, the opening words of verse 13 are a command: "Stay on the alert." The verb is a present imperative of *gregoreo*. As a present imperative, *gregoreo* probably can be best understood as meaning to *continue to be on the alert*. Jesus is not exhorting this group of people to come to saving faith but to express that saving faith (by means of servitude) in such a way that they may be saved from loss of reward. The exhortation is a call to faithfulness, not an invitation to come to faith.

To be sure, a lack of faith on the part of the servant who buries his talent (in the Matthean parable) and on the part of the servant who hides his mina (in the Lukan parable) is evidenced by their behavior and confessed by their own lips. These servants explicitly identify the reason they bury their talent as fear, which is the opposite of faith (Mt 25:25; Lk 19:21). Such lack of faith does not mean, however, that such servants are unbelievers. Christians are supposed to walk by faith, yet they may fail to do so. Some Christians walk in fear rather than by faith. If believers do not walk by faith, they will suffer loss of rewards. The Greek word used of the *faithful* believers in these parables is *pistos*. This word can also be used to describe someone who has *faith*. In these two contexts, *pistos* probably has both meanings—*faith* and *faithfulness*—since *pistos* is contrasted with fear as well as equated with loyal service. The working/living faith pictured by the Lord in these two parables is a rewards issue. Faithful faith results in a reward. As the Lord clarifies in the parable of the minas, wimpy faith only results in the salvation of one's life (picturing the free gift of eternal life). Praise God that a timid faith can save from hellfire. Still, it takes a serving faith to save from the outer darkness.

The servant with timid faith believes a number of things. He believes that his master is coming back. Additionally, he believes that it would be better to hide the talent rather than spend it, evidently because he believes that his master will hold him accountable. Moreover, he even shows an *obedience of faith* in that he accepts the entrustment. So in both parables there are multiple indications of faith even on the part of those who are unfaithful. But it is not a victorious or virtuous faith. Their faith is fearful rather than watchful.

Jesus indicates that if we are watchful we can prevent the thief from coming in the night and breaking into our house (Mt 24:42-43). Does this mean that we can prevent the rapture by looking for it? Hardly! Rather, if we are diligently on guard, the event of the rapture and resulting *bema* will not have a devastating impact on our earthly lives. The results of the rapture will be exhilarating to those prepared for it but excruciating to those who are not. One normally does not look forward to a thief coming and breaking into one's house and taking everything one has! It is understandable that not all Christians look forward to the rapture. Parabolically speaking, the *bema* rapture either will result in God taking everything you have or rewarding you with everything He has! To use a Christmas illustration, one works to prevent thieves from breaking into one's house, not to prevent Santa Claus from doing so. God knows if you have been naughty or nice, so be good for the sake of the potential rewards.

Believers Addressed by Warning

Second, as already noted, since the *you* addressed in the warning is addressed to Peter, James, John, and Andrew (cp. Mt 24:3 with Mk 13:3), the warning of these parables is for those who genuinely are saved.

> ³And as He was sitting on the Mount of Olives opposite the temple, **Peter and James and John and Andrew** were questioning Him *privately*, ⁴"Tell us, when will these things be, and what will be the sign when all these things are going to be fulfilled?" ⁵And Jesus began to say to *them*, "See to it that no one misleads **you**." (Mk 13:3-5)

> ³And as He was sitting on the Mount of Olives, **the disciples** came to Him *privately*, saying, "Tell us, when will these things be, and what will be the sign of Your coming, and of the end of the age?" ⁴And Jesus answered and said to *them*, "See to it that no one misleads **you**....¹³Be on the alert then, for **you** do not know the day nor the hour." (Mt 24:3-4; 25:13)

The warnings are addressed to His disciples (Peter, James, John, and Andrew), who are questioning Him privately. Thus, it is inconceivable that the warning about being unworthy slaves is addressed to any other than those who genuinely are saved.

Believers Today Do Not Know That Day

Third, the believers living during the time of the tribulation will know the precise day that Jesus will return with the mathematical certainty. Although Mt 25:13 is a transitional verse with imperatival applicability to believers living in the future to be prepared, the unknown timing of His coming is an interpretational limitation that is only relevant to those living in the present church age. The argument that the Lord will shorten the number of days of the tribulation is a miscalculation of the meaning in Mt 24:22 and Mk 13:20. These days prophetically have been shortened to 1,260 days. *

Believers Are His Own

Fourth, to whom is Jesus referring when He identifies these three slaves as His *own* (Mt 25:14)? Does Jesus refer to the lost or to the saved as His *own*? Surely Jesus' description of believers as His *own* sheep in Jn 10:3-4,14 is the manner in which He identifies those who belong to Him by faith. He calls them His *own*. All three slaves are equally His *own*. The slave who receives one talent is just as much His *own* as the other two. Again, this is conclusive evidence that the unworthy slave is one of the elect—*His own*.

Believers Are Called Slaves

Fifth, whom do the Lord's *slaves* (*doulos*) represent in the NT? Although it would be presumptuous to assume that the term *slave* necessarily refers to someone who is *saved*, nevertheless it is in accord with exegetical conclusions elsewhere to note that whenever someone is affirmed to be a slave of the Lord in the NT that person's status as one of the elect is also implicitly confirmed.† The NT never pictures the Lord's *slave* as someone who is lost. The interpretation that the Lord is using slaves to

---

* Additionally, some interpreters believe the length of the days themselves will be shortened on the basis of Rev 8:12 and Amos 8:9 so that a day will not take the full 24 hours. Regardless of whether the expression means that the days are shortened prophetically or temporally, they will not be shortened numerically. The fact that the time of the Lord's return is unknown means that we can know with certainty that it is addressing believers living in the present time period.

† The slaves in Mt 13:27 picture the elect—albeit probably elect angels.

picture saved believers in this parable is in accord with NT usage. The implementation of this observation is not reading an epistolary usage back into the gospels; rather, this interpretation finds that the epistolary usage may be traced back to the Lord Himself in that He regards believers as His slaves and His slaves as believers. Those attempting to neutralize the term *slave* so as to use it indiscriminately as referring jointly to both believers and unbelievers will have to assume the burden of proof. Let them prove that the slave is unsaved.

Believers Are Entrusted

Sixth, to whom does the Lord *entrust* His work (in Mt 25:14)—to the lost or to the saved? Granted, there are unsaved people who have taken positions of leadership in the churches. But that is the point; they have **taken** these positions; these positions have not been **given** to them by the Lord. If a lost person has taken the role of the pastor, it is not because the Lord has called him to that position. The point of this parable is not that some people hold positions they should not be occupying. Rather, it is that some people who are in their proper God-given positions are not doing their God-given duty. Does the Lord impart these talents to the lost **and** saved? No. These are not natural talents, but spiritual talents to be used in His work. The Lord gives His spiritual talents (such as spiritual gifts) only to those who genuinely are saved. With the receiving of such gifts comes the responsibility of using them profitably. To what would the departure of the Master correspond in Mt 25:15? It naturally would refer to the ascension at which time Jesus left believers in charge of His work. The Great Commission is a mission given by the Lord to believers, not to unbelievers. When the Lord departed, He entrusted believers with the task of making disciples and gave each believer at least one spiritual gift to use in that task. He did not entrust the lost with the Great Commission nor give unbelievers spiritual gifts to use in His work. The unworthy slave must be one of the elect since he is so entrusted.

Some think that the unfaithful slave refers to a lost Jew who ultimately is removed from his covenantal relationship with God. In response it may be asked, "Did Jesus intend to say that He would be entrusting the lost Jews with the work of His kingdom when He returned to His Father?" Of course not. The text describes an unfaithful believer who ultimately is removed from his position of service to God. The question pertains to service, not to relationship. Costly-free pastors who contend otherwise and claim that a saving relationship is forfeited because of poor performance are advocating a performance-based relationship.

Contrary to costly-free pastors, what is lost is not salvation from eternal damnation but the opportunity to serve. Certainly those in hell lose any opportunity to serve God, but why presume that the service or lack thereof represents that of a severed relationship? After all, if the service of

Chapter 2. The Nature of Rewards

the other two slaves represents that of genuine believers serving the Lord, then it would be natural to take the lack of service represented by the third slave to picture the failure of genuine believers in serving God. This would also coincide with the teaching of the NT in which it is possible to lose one's crown (Rev 3:11), to lose one's reward (2Jn 1:8), and to suffer loss at the *bema* (1Cor 3:15). Further, in the twin parable of the minas, the taking away of the mina is contrasted, rather than equated, with the forfeiture of life (Lk 19:24-26). In distinction to the enemies who lose their lives, the friend loses his mina. Rewards are forfeitable; the gift of eternal life is not forfeitable.

Granted, the Jewish people (i.e., those related to God by physical birth under the old covenant in the past) were the ones who originally "**were entrusted**" with the oracles of God" (Rom 3:2). (Note the past tense.) Some object that since not all Jews under the old covenant were saved (yet the Jewish race was entrusted with the oracles of God), not all those entrusted in the present dispensation necessarily are regenerate either. Supposedly, mere professing believers are entrusted with the gospel as part of the covenant community.

In response to such an objection, note that in the new dispensation it is not professing believers but genuine believers (who are related to Him under the new covenant which entails a circumcision of the heart rather than of the flesh) to whom the Lord entrusts Himself and His work. The NT is replete with conceptual parallels, which also have been rendered by the NAS as *entrusted* and teach that genuine believers are the ones entrusted with this stewardship (1Cor 9:17) of the gospel ministry (Gal 2:7; 1Thess 2:4; 1Tim 1:11; 1Tim 6:20; 2Tim 1:14; Tit 1:3). In fact, one does not have to wait until the present dispensation to find this transition. Jesus "was not entrusting Himself" to new Jewish converts even during the earliest stages of His ministry (Jn 2:24). Costly-free pastors who misperceive Jesus as entrusting lost Jews (based on covenantal relationship with the Jews) in this Matthean parable portray the Lord as teaching something contrary to His own practice (and Matthew as recording something contrary to NT usage). During His earthy ministry, Jesus was not even entrusting new, regenerate, Jewish converts with fuller intimate revelations of Himself. To claim that these parables show that He is going to entrust unregenerate Jews with the future stewardship of His kingdom message is ridiculous. Either Jesus does not practice what He preaches, or costly-free preachers misunderstand what Jesus teaches.

The latter is the provable state of affairs. Jesus had already announced the transference of stewardship away from the Jews earlier: "Therefore I say to you, the kingdom of God will be taken away from you, and be given to a nation producing the fruit of it" (Mt 21:43). He now pictures that reality parabolically. Jesus is not depicting a stewardship in the old economy (in the parable of the talent and other related parables). Rather, He is speaking futuristically in anticipation of the stewardship in which believers in Him would find themselves in the new dispensation. Paul and Barnabas ran headlong into the reality of this situation and "spoke out boldly and said, 'It was necessary that the word of God should be spoken to you [Jews] first; since you repudiate it, and judge yourselves unworthy of eternal life, behold, we are turning to the Gentiles'" (Acts 13:46).

The Jews proved themselves to be unworthy stewards of the message of eternal life. This message has now been given to the church. It is no longer the Jewish race who proclaims the message of God. A new race has been chosen: "But you [believers] are a chosen race, a royal priesthood, a holy nation, a people for God's own possession, that you may proclaim the excellencies of Him who has called you out of darkness into His marvelous light" (1Pet 2:9). The stewardship has been removed from Abraham's physical descendants and given to his spiritual descendants—to born-again believers—to those who are under the new covenant. The stewardship correspondingly pictured in the parable of the talents is that of a regenerate, new covenant believer.

An objection might be made at this point, in response to the statement made above, that Jesus did not entrust Himself to new believers (Jn 2:24). The effect of this objection would be to note that if Jesus did not entrust new believers, then He did not entrust all believers. Therefore, it could be claimed by detractors that the talent cannot represent the regeneration of all believers. Granted, this is a straw-man argument at this point, as this is merely a hypothetical objection, so there is little need to spend much time responding to it. Nevertheless, in following the NT practice of dealing with perceived potential reactions of hypothetical objectors, a brief response is permissible.

First, the talent does not represent regeneration. Therefore, what is lost is not regeneration. What is lost is stewardship (which is a form of rulership). A rewards issue rather than a salvific matter is at stake. The talent represents an entrusted stewardship for those who have already experienced regeneration. Second, the primary application is not to new believers but to those who have been entrusted with this stewardship over a sufficient period of time so as to have been reasonably expected to produce a return. These stewards do not picture someone saved a day before the rapture being thrown into the outer darkness because he did not produce a major return before the rapture. The parable focuses on the accountability of those who have had time to use their talents to produce a return. This observation, however, is not an invitation to slothfulness on the part of new believers. New believers can be powerful witnesses to their old friends. For example, Zaccheus is a picturesque example of a new believer immediately setting out to earn major rewards.

Nevertheless, the parabolic focus is on the responsibility incurred with time. The more time you have, the greater the expectation of a return. Naturally, those believers who have been in the Lord's service for ten years

Chapter 2. The Nature of Rewards

would be expected to have produced more return than those who had only been believers for ten days.[3] In the parallel passage already addressed, Jesus says, "Who then is the faithful and sensible slave whom his master put in charge of his household to give them their food at the proper time?" (Mt 24:45) Mature believers have a responsibility to immature believers (i.e., to members of the household) to help them mature rather than slap them around. The slave put in charge of the other slaves is the one concerning whom that parable focuses its attention.

The warning in the parable concerning the sensible steward in Mt 24:45 is first and foremost addressed to those in places of leadership in the church. Pastors who fail to feed the immature flock with sound kingdom doctrine and who then abuse those who attempt to do so certainly are going to have much for which to answer. Just as 1Cor 3:11-15 has primary application to the pastor and only secondary application to the general church membership, so the parable concerning the sensible steward has primary application to those entrusted with positions of responsibility in the Lord's house. That parable shows an entrustment according to *maturity*—not all were entrusted. (This would correspond to the phenomena encountered in Jn 2:24.) The present parable concerning the talents shows an entrustment according to *ability*—not all were entrusted equally. The related parable of the minas shows entrustment according to *identity*—all were entrusted equally. These parables form a composite picture of genuine believers according to their identity, ability, and maturity in Christ. To assert that those so entrusted are not genuine believers in Christ is absurd.

Believers Can Hide Their Gifts and Nature

Seventh, the unworthy slave *hid* his talent (Mt 25:18). This negative example also indicates the genuineness of the relationship. After all, you cannot hide something you do not have. A saved person can keep his devotion to Jesus secret. For example, the Gospel of John implicitly and explicitly refers to those who believed in Jesus but who would not confess Him (cf. Jn 2:23-24; 12:42-43; 19:38).[*] The contexts of these passages demand that the regeneration of these believers be accepted. Jn 19:38 is particularly interesting since the same verb (*krupto*) used to describe Joseph of Arimathea is used to describe the unworthy slave who *hid* the talent. Joseph was a hidden disciple, that is, he hid his devotion to Jesus. He was regenerate but hid his relationship to his Master. Luke (11:33) uses the noun form of this word, saying that no one who lights a lamp puts it in a *hidden place* (*kruptos*). Compare this with the similar passage in Mt 5:14-16, where

---

[*] See "Carnal Believers in GJ" in *Believe: An Aspectual and Metaphorical Analysis from the Gospel of John*.

Jesus (after making this statement) said, "Let your light shine." The application is that you **should not** hide *your light*. If it were impossible for regenerate believers to hide their light, then the exhortation would be pointless. Therefore, although it is possible for those who are not really saved to hide their devotion to Christ, this possibility is not what concerned the NT writers, as is evident in the way they use this word to describe the danger of **regenerate** believers hiding their light in terms of hiding their devotion to Christ. Thus, it is very probable that this is the same concern in the parable of the talents.

Illustration 12. Some Christians Hide It

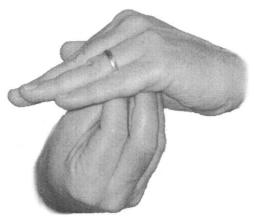

This parable challenges Christians not only to sing but also to put into practice the children's song: "Hide it under a bushel? No! I'm going to let it shine." In Mt 5:14-16 what is in danger of being hidden is one's regenerate nature, that is, what we are as believers. "You **are** the light of the world. A city set on a hill cannot be *hidden* [*krupto*]....Let your light shine." What Joseph of Arimathea hid was not merely his devotion but his regeneration. The same should be concluded concerning the worthless slave. He hid the fact that he had been entrusted with a regenerate nature.

The probability that this aspect of the parable denotes the regenerate nature of the unworthy slave increases to the point of certainty if it is acknowledged that what is hidden is not mere devotion but regeneration. The light that we hide is not merely our devotion. Light is not merely something we do; it is something we are. As Paul beautifully states in Eph 5:8-9, we are light, and thus we should walk in light by manifesting the fruit of the light in what we do. Paul's exhortation in that context makes it clear that Christians may fail to display their regenerate nature in proper action. Proper fruit is not inevitable; it is possible for Christians to hide their light.

Illustration 13. Some Christians Shine It

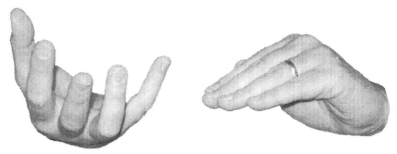

Of course, a person has to have a light before he or she can let it shine. You have to have a talent before you can use it. You have to be regenerate before you can prove it to men. Are you hiding your "little light" under a bushel or in the ground as this unfaithful servant did? He had a talent; he knew it, and His master knew it, but no one else knew it because he hid it.

The conditional securitist may assert this means that the servant lost his regenerate nature when the talent was taken away from him. Yet this is false for at least two reasons. As discussed below, the timing of the loss makes this an unfeasible deduction.* Second, the talent represents the fact that regeneration has occurred. The talent is not regeneration itself.

Spiritual gifts, for example, are distinguishable from the source of those gifts—the Holy Spirit. Although the Holy Spirit is a gift, He is not one of the spiritual gifts which He imparts. It is possible to have the Holy Spirit and yet hide the spiritual gifts which flow from your regenerate nature, but it is not possible to hide the spiritual gifts which would otherwise flow from your regenerate nature without first having a regenerate nature. What is lost is the opportunity to serve. At the very least, the opportunity to use one's gifts in the Lord's service is lost. Quite likely, the spiritual gift itself is taken away also, and as a result the opportunity to use that gift no longer exists. The talent would therefore represent the spiritual gift and its entailing responsibilities and opportunities to serve the Lord.

Believers Judged at This Time

Eighth, as stated previously, the time of this parable is concerned with the present (Mt 25:19). In this verse Jesus purposefully provides a temporal marker, saying that it will occur after a *long time*. This chronological detail

---

* See *Believers' Status Not Forfeitable at This Time*, 30.

reinforces the initial observation made from the other temporal aspects[*] that the time period in view must be His arrival at the end of the current church age. And the delay must be that of the church age. In the Olivet Discourse, Jesus distinguishes between the judgment associated with the rapture and the judgment associated with the revelation. The judgment in view is the Judgment Seat of Christ since it is the one associated with the rapture. Only Christians are evaluated at the Judgment Seat of Christ (as can be seen in 1Cor 3:11-15 and from the fact that only Christians are taken up at the rapture). Thus, if it is accepted that the time period involved is the church age, then it must also be accepted that this judgment follows the rapture, and this unworthy slave is a genuine believer since only believers are dealt with at the Judgment Seat of Christ.[4]

Illustration 14. Distinction in Judgments

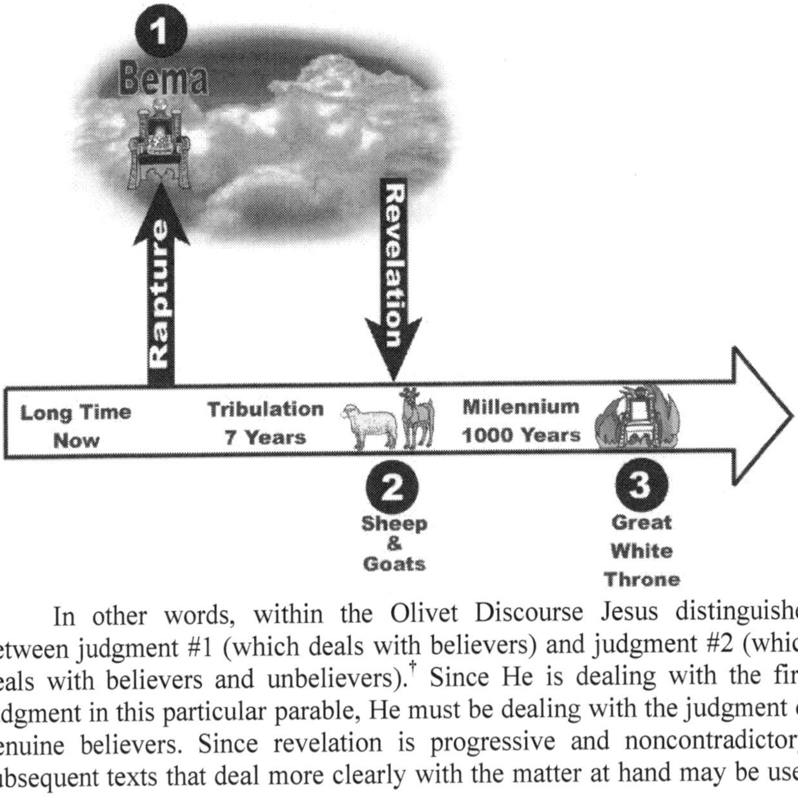

In other words, within the Olivet Discourse Jesus distinguishes between judgment #1 (which deals with believers) and judgment #2 (which deals with believers and unbelievers).[†] Since He is dealing with the first judgment in this particular parable, He must be dealing with the judgment of genuine believers. Since revelation is progressive and noncontradictory, subsequent texts that deal more clearly with the matter at hand may be used

---

[*] See the unknown day or hour of v. 13 discussed previously and the time of the arrival in v. 27 to be considered subsequently.
[†] The Great White Throne Judgment (judgment #3) is not dealt with in the Olivet Discourse.

to aid in understanding related texts. Nevertheless, for the sake of those who do not share this view of the last days, let it be pointed out that the time period in question obviously was futuristic when Jesus spoke these words. Jesus is not referring to physical Jews who were His servants in the past and who belonged to Him by virtue of their past covenantal relationship with Him. He is referring to futuristic Jews who would be His own in the future and who thus would have a saving relationship with Him in that time period, which anticipates the Pauline concept of spiritual Jews (i.e., believers)—if one must insist on thinking of these servants as Jewish servants.

The Lord is not referring to elect Jews in general, much less to elect Jews during the tribulation period. This parable depicts the reality announced by Mt 21:43. The opportunity to earn the *kingship* (*basileia*) of heaven has been taken away from the Jewish people and given to those who produce the fruits of the kingdom. Rulership of that kingdom is contingent upon fruit production. Even if *basileia* is translated spatially as *kingdom* rather than experientially as *kingship* in Mt 21:43, being given a kingdom entails more than mere entrance into that kingdom. The only way one can be given a kingdom is as a king. The production of these fruits is required for kingdom rulership, not for kingdom entrance. Believers are being exhorted to produce fruits of the kingdom of God so that they may inherit positions of rulership within that kingdom. Just as Jews in the past failed to obtain this rulership they so desperately craved, so Christians in the present will fail to obtain it if they fail to produce the necessary fruits. The potential rulership of God's kingdom is *taken away* (*airo*) from God's people, whether they be those related to Him under the old covenant or the new covenant, if they do not produce the necessary fruits (Mt 21:43; 25:28-29). The parable of the outer darkness shows that the same thing that happened to the Jews in the past can happen to believers in the future if they do not produce the necessary fruits. Kingship (i.e., being given the kingdom) is conditioned on the fruits one produces. Having a covenantal relationship with God, whether it be old or new, does not guarantee the production of such fruits.

Believers Have Identical Relationships

Ninth, each of these three slaves has an identical relationship with *his Master* (Mt 25:20). Is this a judgment to determine if they are **genuine** servants? No. It is a judgment to determine if they are **faithful** servants. All three are judged on the same basis—works. This is not a judgment to see if they are believers but workers. This is not a judgment to see if they are genuine believers but to see if they are faithful believers. The one who has his talent taken away has the identical relationship to *his Master* as the other two who are rewarded. In the case of each of the three servants, the same relationship is affirmed by the same words—*his Master* (Mt 25:21,23,26). The purpose of this judgment is not to question their relationship but to question their workmanship. Since the nonelect do not have the same relationship to the Lord that the elect do, this unworthy slave must be one of the elect since he has an identical relationship to his master as the faithful servants.

Because the context of Jesus' first statement regarding the outer darkness (in Mt 8:12) relates it to Jews, some costly-free pastors object that the *sons of the kingdom* thrown into the outer darkness refer to ethnic Israel who considered themselves sons of God because they were Jews. This objection is open to serious questions. Did Jesus intend to say that He would entrust ethnic Jews (and thus lost Jews or perhaps even the lost in general) with the work of His kingdom when He returned to His Father? Would it not be more reasonable to presume that He would entrust the work of His kingdom to believers rather than unbelievers? Naturally, the King is only going to give the kingdom to His sons. Where does the NT ever teach that the unregenerate may be regarded as *sons* of the King (i.e., sons of God)? Granted, *son* is not a technical term for *sons of God*, much less for believers. The word must be interpreted in its context. Still, the present context demands that these entrusted slaves of this future period representing the church age must represent believers.

Jesus contrasted sheep with goats, wheat with tares, and friends with enemies (i.e., citizens) on various occasions when He wanted to make a contrast between the lost and saved. This is not to say that Jesus always used such sharp contrasts in terms of nature or relationships when presenting such distinctions. Indeed, He contrasted good fish with bad fish—fish with fish. On the other hand, these contrasts of fish with fish and sons with sons and seed with seed do not prove that such contrasts are always between the lost and saved. In the parable of the soils, three of the contrasted soils picture soil in which belief is implicitly affirmed (in the Lukan version) and life was imparted in the form of germinating seed. The parable of the Prodigal Son is best taken as tension between two believers. The costly-free assumption that the only purpose of the tension would be to distinguish the lost from the saved is mere presumption. The purpose could just as easily be to contrast the faithful believers with the unfaithful believers. Since the stress in this parable regarding the servants is on the equality of the relationship and the nature of the service within that identical relationship, one may conclude that it affirms the reality of the relationship in its fullest sense.

One might bolster the costly-free argument by noting that the distinction between the bad fish and good fish is a contrast of the lost with the saved in general (Mt 13:47-50). Thus, this anti-reward argument could be summarized as follows:

1. Fish ≠ saved.
2. Sons ≠ saved.
3. Slaves ≠ saved.

But again, the contextual dissimilarity should not be ignored. The bad fish are not put in charge of anything. The opposite is true of the slaves. Ethnic Jews are not the ones put in charge of the Lord's interadvent work. Although the *children* in Mt 21:28-32 might describe physical descendants of Abraham, the same could not be true of the slaves during the church age.* Jesus' past physical ministry was primarily to Jews, but His present spiritual ministry is not characterized by this limitation. The parable is futuristic and pictures the upcoming church age and is thus not to be taken ethnically. The theme of the parable is dealing with being entrusted with present and future responsibilities as rewards in the kingdom, not merely entering the kingdom. In the context of this parable, it is impossible to consider these slaves as representing the lost. They have the same relationship—that of entrusted servants by their Master. What makes the entrustment genuine is not the integrity of their service but the integrity of their Master. He did, in fact, entrust them, representing the fact that God indeed has regenerated us and placed us in His service—whether or not we serve Him.

Believers Have Received What Was Offered

Tenth, all three servants actually *received* what was offered. Belaboring this point is unnecessary since the entrustment of the stewardship already has been discussed above. Still, it should not go unnoticed that the slave was not only offered the responsibility but actually received it. He appropriated what was offered to him. Those who want to turn this into a salvation issue squarely must face this fact. If salvation is what was offered (and the responsibilities which go along with it), then it only can be admitted that the man received salvation. Rather than do a dance around the passage and say that it concerns salvation issues but the man never experienced salvation, the natural reading of the text should be adopted. The man actually lost what he had received. You cannot lose something you never had. If what is lost is salvation (and corresponding opportunities and responsibilities), then the man lost his salvation. Regardless, what is lost is a reward. For costly-free advocates to equate what was lost with salvation is to make salvation a reward and teach a false gospel of salvation by works.

---

* In contradistinction to the ethnical *children* (*teknon*) who merely have a covenantal relationship with God (in Mt 21:28), the sons (*huios*) of the kingdom (and thus of the King) represent regenerate believers (Mt 8:12; 13:38). *Children* of Abraham are not necessarily saved. Not even all *sons* of Abraham are saved since legalistic sons of Abraham form an exception (Gal 4:22; 30). However, only believing sons of Abraham are classified as *sons of God* (Gal 3:7,26). Thus, there are no exceptions to *sons of God* being saved (whether they are referred to as sons of: God, the Father, the Most High, the Lord, the light, or the kingdom).

Believers' Status Not Forfeitable at This Time

Eleventh, only rewards are forfeitable.[5] The talent is not taken away until this person stands before the Lord in judgment after his Master *arrives* (Mt 25:27). The only way conditional security can adequately explain the chronology of this taking away is if the talent represents a relationship equatable with salvation. Yet the timing of such a taking away proves too much for conditional security.

Only the saved are in a position to lose their salvation. Those who were never saved to begin with never had a relationship to lose. Even if such a relationship were forfeitable, the loss of the gift of eternal life would have to occur beforehand. If you stand before the Lord in judgment and possess eternal life, your name will be found in the Book of Life, and you will be allowed into heaven. The Lord does not examine the Books of Works and then strip you of eternal life or erase your name from the Book of Life if you do not measure up. Not even conditional security is that barbaric. The timing of the removal disqualifies conditional security from serious consideration, leaving only a rewards understanding as the natural interpretation of the passage. The timing of the removal (which occurs after the master's arrival) presents a problem even in the theology of those who do not hold to the above *eschatology*.*

These servants had a servant-master relationship with their master before being entrusted with the talent. The talent represents stewardship, not relationship. The slave thrown into the outer darkness was a slave both before being entrusted with the talent and after being stripped of the talent. Although his fellowship and stewardship most certainly changed, his relationship with his master did not change.

Believers Can Suffer Loss

Twelfth, what does the servant lose out on when his talent is *taken away*? Joy (Mt 25:21,23,30) and ruling authority over his master's house (Mt 25:28). Believers certainly can suffer loss of rewards (1Cor 3:11-15). And this must be the type of loss being described here. If what is lost is eternal salvation, as conditionalists pose, then eternal salvation from hell is by works and is not eternal, a supposition which is false on both accounts. Therefore, what is lost is not salvation from eternal damnation. If Christians do not take up their crosses and follow Jesus in discipleship, they will lose their souls (i.e., the eternal value of their earthly lives), not the regeneration of their spirits or their salvation from hell (Mt 16:24-27). Their earthly lives

---

* The word *eschatology* is derived from the Greek word, *eschatos* (last), and refers to the doctrine of the last days (i.e., the end of time) and thus to the millennial and eternal states.

will not have any lasting value in terms of rewards. Believers who do not take advantage of their opportunity to serve the Lord now will find that opportunity to serve Him taken away and given to others. The loss of the ability to serve is a punitive response based on performance.

We serve God now as slaves in order that we may serve Him then as kings. Believers who refuse to serve Him now as slaves will find their opportunity to serve Him then as kings taken away and given to others. Only servants can become servant-kings. By failing to become a servant-king, poor servants lose the capacity to show that they were ever entrusted servants to start with.

Believers Can Be Cast Out

Thirteenth, is it so strange that Jesus talks about believers being *cast out* in Mt 25:30? Earlier, in Mt 5:13, Jesus warned believers about being cast out as worthless salt. And indeed, a day or so after saying this again in Mt 25:30 about worthless slaves, Jesus again warns genuine believers about the danger of being cast out in Jn 15:6 as worthless branches. In these passages, worthless believers are pictured as worthless—salt, branches, and slaves—to be cast out. Nevertheless, it is possible for lost people to be cast out as well. The occurrence in Luke 13:28 marks the single time this word (*ekballo*) is used to describe the eschatological judgment that happens to the unregenerate. The other times it is used of eschatological judgment, it is used to describe what happens to the elect (Mt 8:12; 22:13; 25:30).

It might be argued that these people in Mt 25:30 cannot be believers because Jesus said that He would never cast a believer out (Jn 6:37). But it must be asked, "What does the expression mean in that context?" In the context of Jn 6:37, not being cast out is obviously a guarantee of eternal security, not a guarantee of eternal rewards. Being cast out of the wedding feast in the kingdom is one thing; being cast out of the kingdom itself is quite another. In effect, Jn 6:37 promises believers that they will not be cast out of the kingdom. It guarantees them that they will not experience the casting out described by Lk 13:28. It does not guarantee them that they will not experience the casting out in Mt 8:12; 22:13; 25:30. The *casting out* in these Matthean passages has nothing to do with eternal security. In contrast to Lk 13:28, none of the outer darkness passages specifies that it is the kingdom itself from which they are cast. Instead, it is some event or experience within the kingdom from which they are excluded rather than from the kingdom itself. Being guaranteed that one will not be an outcast in terms of salvation from hell does not guarantee that one will not be an outcast in terms of rewards in heaven.[6]

Believers Are in the Outer Darkness

Fourteenth, this term *outer darkness* is used exclusively by Matthew in his gospel and occurs three times (Mt 8:12; 22:13; 25:30). But what is Jesus' normal designation for hell in Matthew? It is hell of fire, eternal fire, and furnace of fire (see Mt 5:22; 13:40,42,50; 18:8-9; 25:41). In contrast to these hell-fire passages, none of the three usages of outer darkness identifies it with fire. The term *outer darkness* is used exclusively concerning the *bema* judgment of believers in all three parables. Additionally, in the parable of the virgins, the five foolish virgins left standing in the darkness outside are not pictured as being dragged off and thrown into a fire.

In the second passage on the outer darkness, being cast into the outer darkness is pictured as being cast outside of a wedding feast that a king gave for his son which took place at night.

> ^{11} But when the king came in to look over the dinner guests, he saw there a man not dressed in wedding clothes, ^{12} and he said to him, "Friend, how did you come in here without wedding clothes?" And he was speechless. ^{13} Then the king said to the servants, "Bind him hand and foot, and cast him into the outer darkness; in that place there shall be weeping and gnashing of teeth." (Mt 22:11-13)

Therefore, picturing this exclusion as being cast outside the king's castle or palace (not outside the king's kingdom) is appropriate to the imagery conveyed by Jesus' palace parable.*

Believers May Weep and Gnash Their Teeth

Fifteenth, the result of failing to serve is *weeping* (Mt 25:30). In the preceding context of 24:51 concerning servanthood, weeping and gnashing of teeth also refers to the experience of an unfaithful believer. Although the phrase *weeping and gnashing of teeth* can refer to the experience of the lost for failing to **believe**, it can also refer to the experience of the saved for failing to **serve**. Therefore, the expression itself *weeping and gnashing of teeth* is biblically inconclusive as to whether or not the saved or lost are in view. The objection that there will be no tears in heaven because the Lord will wipe away those tears is self-contradictory. Obviously, if there were no tears there, then there would be no tears for Him to wipe away.

---

* For possible historical backdrop to this palace parable about the outer darkness, see *Appendix 2. Enochian Darkness*, 125.

Summary

As summarized in the chart below, no reasons have been found for assuming that the unworthy slave is definitely lost. As a matter of fact, there is not even a single reason to assume he is probably lost. There are only two reasons for thinking he might possibly be lost in the light of NT usage, but, as always, the context is the determining factor. And in this context, there are four reasons to presume he is probably saved. And most importantly, there are nine reasons for believing that the unworthy slave is definitely saved. The only reasonable conclusion is that this man was not lost. He was cast into the darkness outside the palace, not outside the kingdom.

Illustration 15. The Unworthy Slave of Mt 25:13-30

Detail #:	1st	2nd	3rd	4th	5th	6th	7th	8th	9th	10th	11th	12th	13th	14th	15th
Verse #:	13	13	13	14	14	14	18	19	20	24	27	28	30	30	30
Detail:	alert	you	do not know time	His own	slaves	entrusted	hid	long time	their master	received	arrival	take away	cast out	darkness	weeping
1. Definitely saved	✓	✓	✓	✓		✓		✓	✓	✓	✓				
2. Probably saved					✓		✓					✓		✓	
3. Possibly saved													✓		✓
4. Probably lost															
5. Definitely lost															

Probability Ranking

- **Definitely saved:** the statement *never* refers to the lost in the NT, and it is inconceivable that it could do so.
- **Probably saved**: the statement *could conceivably* refer to the lost, but it is never used that way in the NT.
- **Possibly saved**: the statement *sometimes* refers to the saved and sometimes to the lost in the NT.
- **Probably lost**: the statement *could* conceivably refer to the saved, but it is never used that way in the NT.
- **Definitely lost:** the statement *never* refers to the elect in the NT, and it is inconceivable that it could do so.

Chapter 3.
The Nature of the Spirit's Fruit

Root Determines Fruit

Costly-free pastors frequently appeal to *fruit as necessary proof of salvation*. Such *prove-it* pastors believe that one cannot get into heaven apart from a life of good works. Root is said to determine fruit. Therefore, if you do not have the necessary fruit, you do not have the corresponding root. Fruit proves root. According to such preachers, if your life does not visibly manifest good fruit, then you do not have the root of regeneration. Entering heaven is impossible without the proper fruit, that is, without good works. Salvation from hell is ultimately co-dependent upon regeneration and upon the necessary subsequent quality and quantity of one's practical sanctification. Practical sanctification validates justification and is necessary for glorification according to such ***proveitists***.[*]

Fruit of the Spirit

After preaching sequential sermons saying that a person who lives a fleshly life described in Gal 5:19-21 is lost, one such costly-free pastor, in his follow-up sermon on the fruit of the Spirit in Gal 5:22-23, said that Christians spend way too much time in the vice list of Gal 5:19-21. But if the spiritual fruit describes the saved and if the fleshly list describes the lost, how could this preacher use both passages to describe someone who is saved? After claiming that the vice list characteristics prove whether or not one is saved, this proveitist pastor nullified his own argument by turning around and acknowledging that even he had a problem of spending too much time living like the lost people described in Gal 5:19-21! He wished that he could spend more time living in Gal 5:22-23. Yet he regards himself to be a Christian and admits that when Christians live in the flesh, they will experience the deeds of the flesh described by the vice list.

Illustration 16. Lost or Saved?

---

[*] *Proveitists* is a coined abbreviation for *prove-it-tists*: advocates of prove-it theology.

Such sermons try to import the saved back into the description of those who are lost. This costly-free interpretation leads to inextricable problems. How much time can one spend in the vice list of vv. 19-21 before it is determined that one is lost? His follow-up sermon on spiritual fruit blasted his own previous sermons on the vice list. The rocking horse was in full motion. In the follow-up sermon, this costly-free pastor admitted that David was living in the flesh when David sinned against Bathsheba and then persisted in a state of cover-up. The pastor further pointed out that David lost the joy of his salvation (Ps 51:12). Obviously, David was not experiencing the joy of the Spirit during that long stretch of time. Did David lose his salvation? No, according to this proveitist, David just lost the joy of his salvation. The pastor shared this illustration as an OT example of a NT Christian who lives according to the flesh. The problem, then, is that the saved are not only susceptible to the same vices as the lost, but the saved might persist in those vices and fail to have the fruit of the Spirit.

Illustration 17. Lost or Spiritual or What?

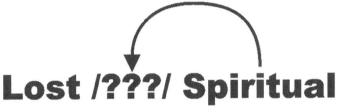

How, then, does one explain the presence of such vice-list Christians and the inconsistency of such costly-free pastors? With a rocking horse of course. On the one hand, this costly-free pastor acted as if all the saved exhibit sufficient spiritual fruit/character so as to prove whether they are saved by the way they live. Supposedly, the lost live fleshly lives, but the saved live spiritual lives, and they can be discerned as lost or saved by the way they live. On the other hand, this pastor acknowledged that the saved may, in fact, live like the lost without being lost. But if the spiritual can live unspiritual lives and not be lost, then an overlapping category is obviously necessitated by such costly-free oscillation. What category would this be?

Illustration 18. Carnal Overlapping

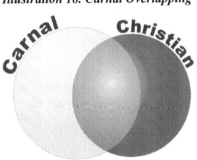

Chapter 3. The Nature of the Spirit's Fruit   *Page 37*

The vast majority of the time, *sarkikos* is translated as *carnal* by the KJV. So this popular designation will be used herein. By the costly-free admission, some people who are saved live fleshly/carnal lives. Would this type of Christian not be called a *carnal Christian*? Many people think so, even some of those among the costly-free camp. Those costly-free pastors who refuse to admit such a category of Christians are doing nothing more than riding an irrational rocking horse.

Illustration 19. The Fruity Rocking Horse

Costly-free pastors are presenting a false dichotomy when they say that the way believers live determines whether or not they are saved and yet acknowledge that the saved can live like the lost. The lost-saved rocking horse breaks under the weight of its own argument.

Illustration 20. The Broken Lost-Spiritual Horse

Trying to determine if believers are lost or saved based on the fruits they produce is an exercise in logical futility once it is acknowledged that saved can behave like the lost. Not only is logical consistency at sake; avoiding teaching a false gospel is at stake as well. Otherwise, entrance into heaven is made costly-free. Rather than throw logical consistency out the window and condition entrance into heaven on the fruits one bears, the Bible injects a third category that categorically breaks the back of the costly-free argument.

> [14]But a **NATURAL** man does not accept the things of the Spirit of God; for they are foolishness to him, and he cannot understand them, because they are spiritually appraised. [15]But he who is **SPIRITUAL** appraises all things, yet he himself is appraised by no man. [16]For who has known the mind of the Lord, that he should instruct Him? But we [apostles] have the mind of Christ. [1]And I, *brethren*, could not speak to you as to spiritual men, but as to **CARNAL** men, as to babes in Christ. [2]I gave you milk to drink, not solid food, for you were not yet able to receive it. Indeed, even now you are not yet able, [3]for you are still carnal. For since there is jealousy and strife among you, are you not carnal, and are you not walking like *natural* men? (1Cor 2:14-3:3; TM)

Three categories of people are seen in this passage: natural, carnal, and spiritual. These carnal believers are described by the apostle Paul as living/walking like the natural/lost according to the dictates of their fleshly desires. These carnal Christians are living lives characterized by *jealousy* (*zelos*) and *strife* (*eris*). Yet these very vices are part of the vice list in Gal 5:20 where Paul warns Christians that those who live like this will not inherit the kingdom of God (Gal 5:21). Astonishingly, costly-free preachers teach that inheriting the kingdom of God is a free gift that is given to believers independent of their performance and then turn around and condition this inheritance on the fruit these believers produce!

Root-Fruit Rhetoric

In his sermons on Gal 5:16-21, the costly-free pastor mentioned above stressed that the control of one's life determines if one will reach heaven. Committing one's life to Christ so that He is in charge was emphasized repeatedly as the way to avoid hell. Translated, this means that Christ must be in charge of your performance in order for you to reach heaven. The reason such costly-free pastors stress that Christ must be Lord of your performance in order for you to reach heaven is because, according to their theology, reaching heaven logically is conditioned on your performance—even though costly-free pastors generally refuse to admit it.

Illustration 21. Root-Fruit Canoe

Not surprisingly, this proveitist claimed that we are not saved because of our good fruit; rather, we bear good fruit as proof that we are saved. According to this proof retort, we bear good fruit because we are saved, not in order to be saved. This evasive maneuver implements the common root-fruit distinction appealed to time and again by such preachers.

This particular proveitist illustrated his point by comparing producing the good fruit to rowing upstream. Merely getting in a canoe and drifting downstream with the flow of the current could be likened to just going with the flow of ungodly influences to produce the negative fruit described by Paul in Gal 5:16-21. Christians need to paddle upstream against the flow of the current. This analogy is splendid to this point. The problem is that the costly-free approach uses this analogy to maintain that we must paddle upstream to be saved from hell. Whoa! Would that not be salvation by works? Of course! Instead of acknowledging the logical outcome of such sermons, however, such pastors invoke the ploy often used by legalists to avoid honestly facing up to the logical implications of such sermons. They claim that we are not saved by the fruit we bear but by the root that produces the fruit.

The most glaring problem with such a ridiculous conclusion in this illustration is that the fruit is the paddle! In such theology the root commitment made in one's heart to change one's performance (by giving control of one's performance to Christ) means nothing if not accompanied by fruitful performance. Even on the basis of his own analogy, this pastor logically was conditioning getting upstream to heaven on paddling upstream. Necessarily, one would have to reach heaven by works.* His suggestion that we are saved by paddling upstream but not saved by the paddling is completely irrational. Obviously, salvation from going downstream is by means of the paddle—by means of the good fruit produced. Exegetically, the same conclusion would be reached from the passage itself.

Paul, writing to Christians, warns them, just as he had already forewarned them: "I warn you, as I did before, that those who live like this [like going downstream in carnal behavior] will not inherit the kingdom of God" (Gal 5:21; NIV). Inheriting the kingdom is conditioned by Paul on the way Christians live. Equating inheriting the kingdom with entering heaven, as this pastor mistakenly did, unmistakably conditions entering heaven on the way Christians live.

Costly-free pastors naturally stress that you must commit your life (i.e., the way you live) to Christ because these pastors and teachers believe that in the end the way you live determines whether or not you will be saved. Amazingly, such preachers stress that you are not saved by works (i.e., by the way you live). Their disclaimer is true, to a point, in that according to their theology you are not **initially** saved by works (i.e., by the way you live). Ultimately, however, their theology makes **final** salvation conditioned on the way you live. Consequently, when their theology is viewed in its entirety (as to what is necessary to be saved from hell), their emphasis that one is not saved by works is completely fraudulent.

---

* The criticism being made herein of costly-free pastors is still accurate even in the case of those costly-free pastors who correctly perceive that the root is regeneration. Regenerative fruit/performance would still be necessary to reach heaven according to their theology. Additionally, Col 3:23-25 explicitly makes the inheritance a reward conditioned on works. Therefore, to equate entrance with inheritance necessarily teaches salvation by works. Yet the root argument, as used by costly-free pastors, is susceptible to even further reproof in that the root they demand from the convert is a commitment to changing performance. The potential convert is told to commit his or her life/performance to Christ in order to be saved from hell. Faith is redefined as commitment of positive performance and repentance regarding negative performance is added to faith, thereby making the commitment to change one's performance the root of the issue. The root is composed dualistically of commitment regarding positive and negative performance; the fruit is composed of the follow through of that performance related commitment—making the whole costly-free schema a performance-based salvation from hell.

Reap What You sow

Some interpreters insist that *prolego* only means *foretell* rather than *forewarn* in Gal 5:21 so that Paul is only reminding and exhorting these believers, not warning them. For sake of cursory argument, let it be supposed for the moment that this is the case:

1. Reminder: I foretell you just as I foretold you that **those who live like this will not inherit the kingdom**.
2. Exhortation: **Christians, do not live like this**.
3. Conclusion: _____?

Strangely, such interpreters have trouble filling in the blank. Presumably, because Paul does not immediately complete his train of thought by specifying what would happen if Christians were to live like this, one cannot fill in the blank but must stop at the exhortatory stage and not follow through to the logical implications of Paul's statement—even though the conclusion comes thundering down a few verses later in Gal 6:7-9! According to these later verses, you reap what you sow—even if you are a Christian! Interpreters who would have us ignore the warning would have us believe the unbelievable: that Paul is merely exhorting Christians to sow good seed without any warning of reaping negative consequences if they do not!

Contrary to such naysayers, this context moves beyond being merely exhortatory to being fully cautionary. Christians are warned that if they live carnal lives, they will not reap eternal life:

> [7] Do not be deceived, God is not mocked; for whatever a man sows, this he will also reap. [8] For the one who sows to his own flesh shall from the flesh reap destruction, but the one who sows to the Spirit shall from the Spirit reap eternal life. [9] And let us not lose heart in doing good, for in due time we shall reap **if** we do not grow weary. (Gal 6:7-9; TM)

This negation expresses a condition: *We (Christians) shall reap **if** we (Christians) do not grow weary*. Reaping eternal life is conditioned on sowing to the Spirit, which Paul has just described as walking by the Spirit (Gal 5:25). Believers must walk by the Spirit in order to sow to the Spirit and to have the fruit of the Spirit. In turn, they must have the fruit of the Spirit in order to reap the harvest of eternal life in return. The passage certainly is describing eschatological reaping. Life and death issues are at stake for the Christian. They are the only ones who have the potential to reap eternal life because they are the only ones who have the seed that can result in eternal life. The expression is popular: You have to have money to make money. In terms of investments, that is true. Similarly, in terms of reaping eternal life, you have to have eternal life before you can sow it in order to reap it. Believers already have eternal life as a gift. What is at stake is whether or not they will reap eternal life in the future as a reward. Those believers who live in a carnal manner can kiss their hopes of receiving the crown of life goodbye. They are destroying any hopes they have of inheriting the kingdom.

Costly-free pastors conflate the gift of eternal life with eternal life as a reward and inadvertently make entrance into heaven a reward. Attempting to avoid the obvious conditionalism in the text is a poorly contrived evasive maneuver. Paul's argument compels one to move forward to the logical conclusions of his statements and fill in the blank with the necessary implication that Paul has left staring them right in the face: <u>Those Christians who live like this will not inherit the kingdom</u>. Those believers who sow according to their flesh will reap destruction. Jointly, Gal 5:21 and Gal 6:7-9 warn believers that carnal Christians' hopes of inheriting the kingdom will be destroyed if they live according to the flesh. Root (i.e., merely having a regenerate nature and seed to sow) does not guarantee fruit (i.e., that one will have the fruit of the Spirit or reap eternal life).

The Nature of the Inheritance

This whole fruit-root assumption that root determines fruit (in terms of the way a believer lives) is exposed as a fiasco when Paul's promise in Col 3:23-25 is considered. Writing again to Christians, Paul exhorts them to work for the inheritance so that they can receive it as a reward for their work:

> Whatever you do, do your **work** heartily, as for the Lord rather than for men; knowing that from the Lord you will receive the **reward** of the **inheritance**. It is the Lord Christ whom you serve. For he who does wrong will receive the consequences of the wrong which he has done, and that without partiality. (Col 3:23-25)

The inheritance is a reward based on works. Therefore, when Paul warns the Galatian Christians that those who live in a godless manner will not inherit the kingdom, he is dealing with a reward concept based on works. Paul wants Christians to paddle upstream against the earthly current so that they may receive *the reward of the inheritance.*

Purely-free advocates believe in paddling upstream. But they do not believe in paddling upstream in order to enter heaven. Heaven is a free gift! Purely-free proponents paddle their hearts out for heavenly rewards, not for heaven itself. Entrance into the kingdom is purely free. Inheritance of the kingdom is very costly. The difference is vast.

Those costly-free pastors who equate entrance into heaven with the inheritance of the kingdom logically turn heaven into a reward based on works, even if such costly-free pastors do not acknowledge explicitly the logical outcome of their own insistence.

Illustration 22. Entrance Versus Inheritance

By equating entrance into heaven with the reward of the inheritance, costly-free preachers are making heaven out to be an oxymoron: a free reward given in response to the way they live but not based on their performance.

Illustration 23. Free Entrance and Free Inheritance

The supposition that entrance into the kingdom and inheritance of the kingdom are both free results in an unsustainable position that seeks to exclude carnal believers from heaven based on their performance—even though entrance into heaven was offered to them as a free gift.

Illustration 24. Free Entrance but Costly Inheritance

Once again the solution is simple and biblical: Recognize that entrance into the kingdom is free but the inheritance of the kingdom is costly. Both cannot be free, and free does not mean costly. Entrance into heaven is purely free to those seeking admission. Inheritance of the kingdom, in contrast, is very costly.

Believers are to paddle upstream for the heavenly reward of hearing the Lord say, "Well done, good and faithful slave; you were faithful with a few things, I will put you in charge of many things" (Mt 25:21). Rulership comes with a price tag. We must pay it with faithfulness, not only paddling upstream, but paddling upstream for the right reasons. Entrance into heaven is not conditioned on how well we perform, but our inheritance of the kingdom certainly is. If believers insult the Lord by trying to earn the gift which He has already freely given them, then they fall from grace (Gal 5:4) into *the outer darkness* (which is exclusion from the realm of ruling service to which they otherwise could have aspired).

Chapter 4.
The Nature of the Believer's Fruit

Inherent Merit

Many costly-free pastors equate earning the crown of life with retaining possession of the gift of eternal life. According to the biblical text (Jam 1:12; Rev 2:10), the *crown (stephanos) of life* is a reward earned by perseverance (i.e., by being faithful unto death). According to the Greek dictionary, this victor's crown is an "award or prize for exceptional service or conduct" whose "primary significance as a symbol of exceptional **merit**" (BDAG). But upon whose exceptional service and merit is this victor's crown based? The believer's merit is being lexically affirmed, of course. A reward is not based merely on the merit of the believer's actions, conduct, or service, but also on the believer's godly character—which the believer has further refined by performing godly actions.

Such faithfulness is a fruit of the Spirit (Gal 5:22). Those believers who sow to the Spirit will reap eternal life as a crown of life. Consequently, the fruit of the Spirit in the life of a believer is a character trait that is associated with the believer meriting a reward as a result of this character development. Since these rewards are not based just on our conduct but also on the character traits instilled into us by such conduct, these heavenly rewards must be based, at least in part, on the inherent merit that resides in the virtue of our Christian character. Our very character has been enriched in terms of rewardability because of the merit that such character deserves. To express this truth in a pun, faithful believers inherit the kingdom because of their inherent merit. Inherent merit is inherit merit.[*] This inheritance is based on the inherent merit of our character development.

Peter conditions a rich entrance into the kingdom on the virtue of one's Christian character (2Pet 1:5-11). The Bible also extols the virtue of character by including an extended praise of the *virtuous woman*, saying that "her worth is far above jewels" (Prov 31:10). God assigns a great worth to her virtue. In the same fashion, Peter urges Christian women to focus on developing their inner beauty by letting "it be the hidden person of the heart, with the imperishable quality of a gentle and quiet spirit, which is *precious* in the sight of God" (1Pet 3:4). The word *precious (poluteles)* means "God

---

[*] As noted in the previous chapter, inheriting the kingdom is a reward which surpasses the gift of merely entering the kingdom. According to Paul, among others, such an inheritance is a reward (Col 3:24). See *The Nature of the Inheritance*, 42.

appraises it at high value" (BDAG). This virtue has *great value or worth* (L-N). In other words, such character has high inherent merit in God's eyes. Christians can add inherent merit to their inner character so that their character becomes valuable in terms of being rewardable in the sight of God.

Add Works

Peter stresses the virtue of developing a godly character as the means by which to earn an abundant entrance into the kingdom (2Pet 1:5-11). Peter is not describing merely *faith that works*; rather, he is picturing *faith plus works*. Faith-works is *faith **and** works* The KJV and NKJV translate the key phrase in 2Pet 1:5 as *add (epichoregeo) to your faith virtue*. A number of other translations also render *epichoregeo* as *add*. (*Supplement* and *supply* are also popular translations.)

Illustration 25. Add/Supply Works to Your Faith

Whether *epichoregeo* is translated as *add* or *supply* makes little difference since Peter's supplementation is addition. The important thing to note is that faith comes first, and works are added to this faith by the believer. For this reason, moving from left to right, faith is pictured as the flowerpot, and works are pictured subsequently on the right as the water canister. Character traits are to be added to this initial faith so that this saving faith may grow into a virtuous faith. Many people mistakenly think that since works are secondary, the popular *faith-works* expression necessarily means that works are *derived from* faith or that these works are merely *evidence of* faith rather than an *addition to* faith. Such limitations are false because Peter is talking about expressions of works as necessary additions to faith in order to qualify for a rich entrance into the kingdom.

Illustration 26. Faith + Works

In this Petrine equation, *faith-works* = *faith* + *works*. Saving faith comes first; it is foundational. However, the works added to that initial faith causes it to grow into a faith that God can reward. Adding works to faith (like supplying water to a plant) allows it to grow into a mature form.[7] Believers are to develop a character worthy of reward. Conditionalists who insist that the *faith-works* expression means that works are strictly *evidence of* saving faith completely invert what Peter is saying.

Illustration 27. Works as Evidence of Faith

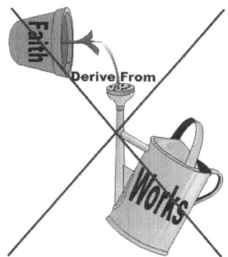

Works are not derived from faith in this passage. Rather, works are added to faith. Petrine addition proves that a theology that must limit its view of faith-works to viewing such postconversional works as mere evidence of faith is false. Peter's perspective makes sense. You have to have faith first before you can add works to it, and you need to add works to it in order to get the desired result. The faith-works perspective that insists that works are only evidence of saving faith is nonsense. Peter is not talking about *faith that works* but *faith and works*. Let Peter speak for himself:

Now for this very reason also, do your very best to
- **add** to your faith, moral virtue
- **and** to your moral virtue, knowledge;
- **and** to your knowledge, self-control,
- **and** to your self-control, perseverance,
- **and** to your perseverance, godliness;
- **and** to your godliness, brotherly kindness,
- **and** to your brotherly kindness, love (2Pet 1:5-7; TM).

Peter makes an addition column by which all these qualities are added by the believers' effort to their initial faith in order to qualify them for an *abundant* entrance into the kingdom in v. 11. Believers are instructed to supply or add something to their initial faith that this initial faith did not have originally. Initial faith has zero virtue in terms of rewards. However, believers can add rewardable virtue to this initial faith and derive a virtuous faith as a result.

Illustration 28. Additions to Faith

<pre>
        Faith
        Moral virtue
        Knowledge
        Self-control
        Perseverance
        Godliness
        Brotherly kindness
      + Love
        Abundant Entrance
</pre>

Faith + works = abundant entrance

According to Peter, if Christians *practice* (2Pet 1:10) adding all these character qualities to their faith, they can have an abundant entrance into the eternal kingdom: "For in this way the entrance into the eternal kingdom of our Lord and Savior Jesus Christ will be *abundantly* [*plousios*] *supplied* [*epichoregeo*] to you" (2Pet 1:11). Peter makes a pun, using the same word for *supply/add* in verse 11 that he did in verse 5. If Christians add these character qualities to their faith, God will add a rich entrance to them. If Christians add this value to their faith, God will add riches to their entrance. If they do their addition, God will do His addition. Believers are already qualified for basic entrance into the kingdom by faith apart from works. But a faith that results in a **rich** entrance into the kingdom requires these additions. *Abundantly* (*plousios*) is also frequently translated as *richly*. This rich entrance into the eternal kingdom is talking about believers meriting **eternal** rewards in heaven because of their earthly performance in building a godly character on earth. Rewards are eternal.

Do Your Best

By means of hard work, Peter enjoins believers to "*do your best* to make your calling and election secure" (2Pet 1:10; TM). The word that Peter uses is s*poudazo* and conveys the idea of *doing your best, working hard, sparing no effort*. Peter used the noun form (*spoude*) to introduce the list in verse 5 when he said to do your best to add moral virtue to your faith. This virtue is added by the believer's hard work, by the believer's effort. To be sure, it is God-enabled effort. Nevertheless, it is the believer's effort (i.e., the believer's hard work) that goes into adding these virtues to the believer's faith. Rewards are based on the believer's works.

Secure (*bebaios*) means to *guarantee*. Believers are to work hard to secure/guarantee their *calling and election*. The realization of their calling and election (in terms of rewards) in achieving a rich entrance into the kingdom is secured or guaranteed by their perseverance, among other character traits. Perseverance is just part of this list. Yet drawing attention to perseverance suffices to show a common fallacy. Those who make perseverance a condition for final salvation from hell have perverted the gospel and inverted the Petrine intent. Those who misconstrue this passage into teaching how believers can be sure of reaching heaven have perverted its faith-plus-works reward into an accursed faith-plus-works gift. Peter is not talking about how to guarantee that believers are genuine believers but how to guarantee that they will be richly rewarded.

Conditional securitists mistakenly think that just because these postconversional works are performed by God's enabling grace that believers can trust in their performance as a condition for reaching heaven and still make it to heaven by claiming that heaven is a free gift that they did not merit. According to the Bible, however, those taking that meritorious path to heaven will find that they have taken a path to hell instead, even if they deny the logically meritorious nature of the path they have chosen. Logical consistency is important because those who *believe that they believe* in a free entrance (when in fact they logically do not actually believe it is free) will be excluded from the kingdom even if they have fooled themselves into thinking otherwise.*

---

* See *Believing That You Believe*, 114 (cf. *Illustration 68. It is Finished If...*, 113).

Activity Not Passivity

Some costly-free advocates are quick to attribute the production of spiritual fruit exclusively to the Spirit and discount any effort on the part of the believer. They do so in order to try and quail any concerns that they are teaching salvation based on the believer's performance. Supposedly, God does it all. God is claimed to be rewarding His own work when He rewards the believer's perseverance in faith. Thus, salvation from damnation is said to be based on God's works rather than the believer's work. God's merit rather than the believer's merit is said to be exclusively in view. In this way, costly-free advocates hope to condition a believer reaching heaven on the believer's works without acknowledging that these works are truly the believer's works.[8]

Illustration 29. Passive Paddling

The canoe, so to speak, practically paddles itself. The believer roots back into his or her canoe and enjoys the ride. God does the paddling after all, not the believer. Let God sweat it. Let go, and let God. You just need to surrender to God's control and trust Him to produce the fruit. No need to blister your hands paddling up the stream. You just lay back and passively abide in Christ and leave the results up to Him. God is the one who does all the work—if you will just let Him.

Such a fairytale view of the Christian life has its advocates, and some costly-free pastors are quick to use this sentiment to their advantage in order to cloak their performance-based view of salvation. Of course, such a view certainly seems at odds with the costly-free view that stresses that believers actively have to paddle upstream rather than passively float downstream.* Evidently, your canoe still has to move upstream in order for you to reach the costly-free heaven, but supposedly you are not the one who has to move it. God moves it by doing the paddling for you.

Even if this mythical view of fruit bearing were accurate, paddling (i.e., postconversion performance) is still made necessary to reach the costly-free heaven. Reaching heaven remains conditioned on fruit, not just root, in such theology. The root of regeneration (i.e., the gift of eternal life) is insufficient to get you to costly-free heaven. Getting to heaven is still by works. Arguing for passive production still ends up with performance-based security.

Illustration 30. Tragic Ending

Not all canoe trips have a happy ending. Two results are possible. Such deluded individuals could passively coast along, doing nothing to move upstream, and actually move downstream in terms of meeting God's expectations regarding performance and character development. Or such individuals might move upstream (in terms of performing in a godly manner) and erroneously attribute any positive results exclusively to God, thinking that they are pleasing God by moving upstream and giving God all the glory, when in fact they logically are trying to work their way to heaven.

Giving God all the glory for trying to work one's way to heaven is not going to fool God into thinking that costly-free advocates of passive fruit production are not trying to work their way to heaven. They may fool themselves into thinking that they are not working their way to heaven, but they will not fool the Lord. God knows that they are still trying to get to heaven by works after He has warned them that they cannot get to heaven by works. Attributing their works to God so that they can still trust in their works to get to heaven does not honor God. It insults Him. He demands that we accept the fact that entrance into heaven is a free gift apart from works.

Peter's description of how spiritual fruit is produced nullifies any such appeal to pure passivity on the part of the believer. If the believer is to develop the character traits being urged by Peter, the believer must be active,

---

* See *Illustration 21. Root-Fruit Canoe*, 39.

indeed very active, in the fruit production process. Biblically, postconversion works are our *works* which we produce through God's *energy*. Paul clearly affirms both his effort and God's enablement: "For God is the one who is internally energizing you both to desire and to be energized according to His good pleasure" (Phil 2:13; TM). "And for this purpose I also diligently labor, agonizingly striving according to His energizing, which energizes me with power" (Col 1:29; TM).

Without delving into the Greek, summation suffices: God provides the energy, but we supply the sweat. We provide the labor; God provides the means and motive for the labor. God provides the energy, but we supply the effort.[9] God is our Helper, but we are God's laborers.[10] By conditioning entrance into heaven on the works which God energizes them to perform or on the fruit which God enables them to produce, costly-free advocates are still conditioning entrance into heaven on their performance and making heaven a reward.

Rewards in heaven are gained by working through the enabling power God provides. The fact that God is working through the believer does not mean that the believer is not working for a reward or what the believer is doing is not a work.

Former Sins

Someone may ask, "What about those believers who lack perseverance (and the other qualities on Peter's list)?" Peter gives an answer: "For he who lacks these qualities is blind or short-sighted, having forgotten his purification from his former sins" (2Pet 1:9). That this person is a believer is clear since his slate was completely wiped clean in regard to *his former sins*. Two fundamental observations are self-apparent: One, the person was a genuine believer since his former sins were forgiven.[*] Two, perseverance is really missing in the lives of some believers. Peter is not dealing with a mere hypothetical possibility.

Why does Peter only mention the purification of this believer's *former* sins? Why not *all* sins? After all, all of a believer's sins are forgiven in regards to going to heaven (Col 2:13). A reasonable proposal, in view of the context, is to suggest that Peter is reminding his Christian readers that when they became Christians and experienced the bath of regeneration (cf. Tit 3:5), this forgiveness only wiped the slate clean for their former sins pertaining to rewards. After that point in time, everything in a believer's life counts toward whether or not that believer will inherit the kingdom with a rich entrance.

---

[*] If Peter had just been talking about provisional forgiveness available to unbelievers, he would not have limited it to past forgiveness.

Oh, to be sure, cleansing in regards to the gift of justification results in the cleansing of all a believer's sins—in regard to entering heaven. Entrance into heaven is unconditionally assured. Yet stressing this aspect of forgiveness would be counterproductive to the reward theme Peter is developing. Peter is not discussing assurance of entering heaven but assurance of richly entering heaven. Assurance of entrance for those who have been cleansed is a given. In contradistinction to this rudimentary forgiveness, Peter subtly is reminding believers that this initial forgiveness only wipes the slate clean in regards to the *bema* for those sins that were committed up until the point in time they became believers. Peter is encouraging believers not to rest on their laurels but to work hard at adding virtue to their initial faith (which is without initial virtue) in order that they may derive a virtuous faith and obtain a rich entrance into heaven as a reward for their resulting conduct and character (2Pet 1:11). The reason their Christian conduct is so important is because it improves their Christian character and thereby qualifies them for rewards in heaven. Heaven itself is a gift and is entered freely. Nevertheless, an abundant entrance into heaven is a reward.

Abide in Me

Advocates of passive productivity are quick to appeal to Jesus' description of how to produce fruit in His vine and the branches analogy:

> ⁴Abide in Me, and I in you. As the branch cannot bear fruit of itself, unless it abides in the vine, so neither can you, unless you abide in Me. ⁵I am the vine, you are the branches; he who abides in Me, and I in him, he bears much fruit; for apart from Me you can do nothing. ⁶ If anyone does not abide in Me, he is thrown away as a branch, and dries up; and they gather them, and cast them into the fire, and they are burned.
> ⁷ If you abide in Me, and My words abide in you, ask whatever you wish, and it shall be done for you. ⁸By this is My Father glorified, that you bear much fruit, and so **prove** to be My disciples. (Jn 15:4-8)

"There you have it," thinks the passive proveitist, "The way you live and the fruit you produce prove whether or not you are saved (abiding in Christ), so you need to abide passively in Christ (and thereby bear much fruit); otherwise, you will be thrown into the fires of hell."

A few elementary observations will suffice for present purposes. First, Jesus commands these believers to abide in Him. He does not promise that they will abide in Him. The nature of such a command is that it cannot be taken for granted that those being commanded necessarily will abide in Him.

Therefore, whether or not one abides in Him (in the sense that *abide* is being used in this context) cannot be used as a necessary indicator as to whether or not one is a believer. Consequently, whether or not a believer produces fruit (as used in this context) is not a given.

Second, what is being proven is whether the believer is a disciple (in the sense being used in this context), not whether one is a believer. The passage is addressed to genuine believers. What is being brought into question by their production is not their regeneration.

Third, discipleship is costly, as even passive advocates admit. By making such discipleship necessary to enter heaven, the passive advocate is subscribing to the contradictory costly-free view of heaven.

Fourth, the Bible entertains the possibility of a believer's work going up in flames at the *bema*: "If any man's work is burned up, he shall suffer loss; but he himself shall be saved, yet so as through fire" (1Cor 3:15). That poorly performing believers are submitted to the fires of judgment is not incompatible with believers suffering loss in terms of God's fiery judgment.

Fifth, deriving a positive outcome is conditioned by Paul on a believer's works, pictured as building upon the foundation of Christ. This building analogy is not a picture of passivity.

Sixth, John's context tells believers how to abide: through activity not passivity. "**If** you keep My commandments, you will abide" (John 15:10). Abiding is **conditioned** on actively keeping Christ's commandments.

Seventh, the injunction that believers *abide* in Christ certainly carries with it the idea of *remaining* in Christ. Interpreting abiding as the necessary condition to escape the fires of hell necessarily conditions salvation from hell on perseverance. Abiding/persevering is not the mere proof of discipleship in such a view, it is the means to escape the fire. The position of the proveitist reduces to interpreting the Jn 15:6 as saying, "**If** anyone does not persevere, he will be cast into hell." Using the text as a proveitist proof text necessarily leads to a security that is conditioned on performance.

Eighth, being fruitful (and thus not withering) is attributed to **perseverance**, not passivity, by Jesus in the parable of the soils. The seed sown on the rocky soil *withers* (*xeraino*) because it lacks sufficient root (Mt 13:6). In this parable of the vine, the Lord conditions not withering on **abiding**: "If anyone does not abide in Me, he is thrown away as a branch and *withers* [*xeraino*]; and they gather them, and cast them into the fire and they are burned" (Jn 15:6; TM). The seed on the good soil bears fruit *by means of perseverance* (Lk 8:15). The two passages are complimentary. Believers are to draw their strength and sustenance from the Lord so that they might persevere in keeping His commandments and thus not be thrown away, wither, and be burned as a result. Not being burned is conditioned on persevering. By equating this burning with hell, passive costly-free advocates are conditioning their salvation on their perseverance—a very active perseverance at that.

Chapter 5.
The Nature of the Soil

Soil determines Fruit

The interpretation proposed by conditionalists for the *parable of the soils*[*] is that the first three soils represent the lost (i.e., those who do not make it to heaven). Prove-it conditionalists argue that these two intermediate soil types refer to those who never were saved. The lack of fruits among the rocky and thorny soils supposedly proves that such people never genuinely believed. *Lose-it* conditionalists argue that the rocky and thorny soils represent those who *lose the gift of eternal life*. Since germination occurred, life occurred. These conditionalists maintain that the life subsequently was lost (i.e., forfeited). Therefore, ***forfeitists*** believe that the gift of eternal life may be forfeited.[†]

In contrast to the proveitist claim that root determines fruits, the proposal herein will be that the soil determines the fruits. Four types of soils are presented in the parable. Unconditional security interprets the germination in the latter three soil types as representing regeneration. Therefore, those represented by these last three soils have eternal life and make it to heaven, despite the poor performance of some of these soil types. Unconditional securitists believe that *even poorly performing believers keep the gift of eternal life*. Thus, ***securitists*** believe that the gift of eternal life is non-forfeitable.[‡] The possession of the gift is unconditional secure.

Illustration 31. The Parable of the Soils (Lk 8:4-15)

	❶ Hard 👎 	❷ Rocky 👍 	❸ Thorny 👍 	❹ Good 👍 
Life	✗	✓	✓	✓
Growth			✓	✓
Mature fruits				✓

---

[*] For sake of simple reference, Jesus refers to the parable as *the parable of the sower* (Mt 13:18). In terms of explanation, however, the focus is on the soils.
[†] ***Forfeitist*** is a coined abbreviation for advocates of lose-it theology.
[‡] ***Securitist*** refers to an advocate of keep-it theology.

The thumbs-up symbol is used to show the agreement between the securitists and forfeitist interpreters that the last three soils represent those who have experienced regeneration. Since only mature fruits are charted, this introductory chart allows the proveitist assumption to go unchallenged that only the forth soil produces fruits. If it is granted that the third soil produces immature fruits (as will be argued below), then the subsequent charts presented herein would be preferable. Both the forfeitist and the securitist interpretations can admit, without any difficulty, that believers can produce fruits and yet fail to persevere sufficiently to produce mature fruits. Proveitists may be reluctant to acknowledge that the third soil produces fruits since proveitists believe that fruits prove whether or not one was ever saved. Obviously, the proveitist position is going to experience difficulty when it admits that its theology does not offer any fruit-based assurance until one reaches a mature state of fruit production. What little illusory assurance is available in the proveitist camp would have to be delayed until one reaches Christian maturity. Under the prove-it-or-you-don't-have-it mentality, immature Christians logically would have to be denied anything remotely approaching absolute assurance that they are genuine believers—if temporary faith and immature fruits are produced by the lost. This biblical text is not the only one that presents such problems for the proveitist group, but it is one of the most picturesque presentations of their problem.

Hard Soil

The parable of the hard soil is the first of the four soils introduced and explained by Jesus: "A sower went out to sow his seed. And as he sowed, some fell along the path and was trampled underfoot, and the birds of the air devoured it" (Lk 8:5). The hard soil never had the seed planted inside it. The seed never germinated or produced life within this soil. This soil represents those who hear the gospel, but the gospel does not penetrate into their hearts, so faith is not produced nor its resultant life. For "faith comes by hearing, and hearing by the word of God" (Rom 10:17). These types of people subsequently forget the gospel. But in this hard soil, there is no faith, life, germination, regeneration, or abiding. Jesus interprets this soil type for us: **"And those beside the road are those who have heard; then the devil comes and takes away the word from their heart, so that they may not believe and be saved"** (Lk 8:12). The implication of Jesus' explanation is that if the seed had remained in the soil, it would have produced faith and therefore salvation. The key to understanding this entire parable is provided in Jesus' introductory explanation. Those who believe are saved: *believe and be saved*.

Chapter 5. The Nature of the Soil

Rocky Soil

In contrast to the hard soil, the other three types of soil receive the word, believe it, and experience its life-giving effect. The rocky soil is the first type of soil to experience the life-giving effect of the word. Jesus describes this life-giving experience as thus: "And other seed fell on rocky soil, and as soon as it **grew up**, it withered away, because it had no moisture" (Lk 8:6). The type of person represented by the rocky soil is someone who receives the word. It is implanted in this person. Absolutely no other legitimate conclusion is possible. The fact that the seed *grew up*, proves that the seed sprouted in the soil and imparted its incipient life-giving property to the soil.

Implanted

The word Jesus uses for *grew up* (*phuo*) is the root of the same word that James uses in Jam 1:21 to describe regeneration as the implanting of the word: "In humility receive the word *implanted*, which is able to save your souls." The word germinated (i.e., it produced life) in this rocky soil. For this reason, the latter three soil types are given the thumbs up symbol to illustrate the fact that these three soils indeed represent the regenerate.

The key word in Jam 1:21 is *implanted* (*emphutos*). It is somewhat ambiguous in the NAS. Is *implanted* an adverb or an adjective? Does the word *implanted* modify *receive* or *word*? Is the word already implanted in these believers or not? Is the verse telling these believers how to receive the word or is it telling them what to receive? This ambiguity does not exist in the Greek text. *Implanted* is definitely an adjective describing *word*. The NKJ version, with greater accuracy and clarity, translates v. 21 as, "Receive...the implanted word." The *word* is already implanted in them. The question is not, "Is the word implanted in them?" but what kind of response or reception will that implanted word have within them now that it has already been implanted in them? Will they be doers of this word that has been implanted in them? In terms of the parable of the soils, what type of soil will they prove to be: rocky, thorny, or good? Will they produce mature fruits? Whether or not they do so is not determined by the root (which they already have), but by their response. They (representing the soil) determine the fruits. The response of the soil determines the extent of the fruits.

The NTME translation (among others) provides an excellent rendition of this aspect of Jam 1:21 by translating it as, "Humbly accept the message that God **has planted** in your hearts, and which can save your souls. Don't only hear the message, but put it into practice; otherwise you are merely deluding yourselves." This rendering correctly points out that the word already has been planted in these believers and consequently indicates that saving their souls subsequently is based on works. (What is at stake in the epistle of James is the salvation of the believer's soul from a merciless judgment at the *bema*, not the salvation of the believer's spirit from hell.)

The significance of this *implanted* word in Jam 1:21 often is overlooked. It recapitulates what already has been stated in Jam 1:18 and is equivalent to 1Pet 1:23. Peter assures his readers "You have been born again not of seed which is perishable but imperishable, that is, through the living and abiding word of God." James likewise assures the readers of his epistle: "In the exercise of His will He brought us forth by the word of truth." James' exhortation in 1:21 to "humbly accept the message that God **has** planted in your hearts" must be understood within its context. The Heavenly Father is using James to tell His children to give this word that already has given birth to them an appropriate reception. It would be just like your earthly father telling you to give your mother a warm welcome, an appropriate response. The question is not whether or not your mother has given birth to you. The question concerns your response to her. The question is not concerning conception but reception. The question is not whether those being addressed are regenerate. James assures these readers that they were born by the word. This assurance is the basis for the exhortation. Assurance provides the basis for fruitful production; assurance does not come as a result of the fruitful production. Contrary to the proveitist camp, James makes assurance a means to fruit production, not the result of fruit production. Assurance is the grounds for performance, not performance for assurance. The question is whether these believers will obey the word which gave them birth. One may ask, "Well what kind of reception is expected?" In light of Jam 1:18, a very clear illustration is possible.

James' epistolary procedure could be likened to your father telling you, "Obey your mother." There is no question as to whether or not she is your mother. On the contrary, the assurance of the fact that she is your mother is the very reason you should obey her. Your obedience or lack of it does not throw your birth into question, but it does raise the issue of discipline. If you fail to obey your mother after your father explicitly has told you to obey her, then you can expect to suffer the paternal consequences. If you fail to obey the word of God that has given you birth, after your heavenly Father explicitly has told you to obey it, then you can expect to suffer the Fatherly consequences. Young children can understand this principle very well: *If you don't obey mom, then look out for dad!* Disobedient children will not save their fannies from a spanking, and disobedient Christians will not save their souls from loss of rewards at the *bema*. Both will emit a squeal of distress.

Whether or not you obey your mother (i.e., the word that gave you birth) does not determine whether you are born of your mother. Whether believers obey God does not determine whether they have been born of God. The fact that spiritual birth occurred should not be thrown into question by poor performance. Birth is the basis for the performance, not the guarantee of it. (Birth/root does not guarantee fruit/performance).

Fall Away

Jesus' explanation in Lk 8:13 confirms the securitist interpretation of the rocky soil in v. 6. The word remains, that is, abides, in the believing soil, although the soil does not remain in a believing state: "And those on the rocky soil are those who, when they hear, receive the word with joy; and these have no firm root; **they believe for a while, and in time of temptation fall away**" (Lk 8:13). Those represented by the rocky soil hear the word, receive it, believe it, and experience its initial life-giving properties before they fall away. To be sure, they subsequently *fall away*, but the seed does not *fall out*. This verse confirms that the word produced life (and thus regeneration) in this soil since it had sprouted up. Peter describes it this way: "For you have been born again not of seed which is perishable but imperishable, that is, through the living and abiding word of God" (1Pet 1:23). The seed produced life and remained in the soil. Peter teaches that the new-birth is a result of the seed-producing life. He further depicts this seed as remaining, abiding. Jesus, in the same way, pictures the seed as abiding (remaining) in all but the first soil. In contrast to Lk 8:12, where the word was taken away before it produced life, the word remains in 8:13, where it was received and believed. Likewise, in Jn 1:12 these two actions—receiving and believing—are synonymous with each other and result in new birth. What is more, the Person who is received in Jn 1:12 is pictured as the Word. In all but the case of the first soil (i.e., the hard ground), the seed (i.e., the word) germinates and remains.

Jesus had already established a clear link between remaining, believing, and salvation in Lk 8:12. Satan takes away the word from the hard soil so that belief would not occur resulting in salvation. Salvation is linked not only with faith but with the seed remaining in the soil. The Lord establishes a contrast between the seed being taken away from the first soil (i.e., the hard soil) and remaining in the other three soils. The seed is not taken from the remaining three soil types. So even if one had nothing else by which to derive one's conclusion, one would anticipate that the remaining soils represent those who are saved. To be sure, those represented by the rocky soil *fell away*, but the word that had been implanted within them was not *taken away*. The word stayed.

Believe and Be Saved

Luke further specifies that the rocky soil represents those who believed (Lk 8:13) and, by means of contrast with the preceding verse, indicates that those who believed would be saved: "The devil comes and takes away the word from their heart, so that they may not *believe and be saved*" (Lk 8:12). The Lukan indication is that salvation is determined by whether one ever believes,[11] not by whether one perseveres in believing, much less by whether one perseveres in producing fruits. Satan must take away the word sown in the heart before it germinates (in regeneration) in order to prevent salvation from occurring. Choking out the fruit production would be insufficient to prevent the life-giving benefits of the seed from being produced within the soil. Sprouts (immature roots) as in the case of the second soil, much less mature roots (as in the case of the third soil), would be sufficient for salvation. Only the first soil (i.e., the hard soil) represents those who never believed and were never saved. The other three types represent those who believed and were saved.

To reiterate, Jesus did not say in v. 12, "So that they may not bear fruits and be saved." Rather, He says, **"So that they may not believe and be saved."** The clear implication is that if they believed, they would be saved. In the next verse, Jesus explicitly says that those pictured in this rocky soil believed, so we are to infer that they were saved, even though they only *believed for a while*: "And those on the rocky soil are those who, when they hear, receive the word with joy; and these have no firm root; they *believe for a while*, and in time of temptation fall away." They believed and thus had eternal life (Jn 6:47). Jesus promises eternal life, not eternal faith. He guarantees that believers would be born of the word. The Lord does not declare that believers will be doers of the word. He assures life (regeneration) in response to saving faith, not fruits.

No criticism is expressed by Jesus regarding quality, nature, or kind of faith experienced by the rocky believer. No disassociation is provided between the faith that is temporary in Lk 8:13 and the faith that results in salvation in Lk 8:12. The unrealized potential faith of 8:12 is realized in the faith of 8:13. The life-giving salvation anticipated in 8:12 is realized in 8:13. Faith is produced, and the germination of salvation results in the rocky soil.

Illustration 32. Duality of Faith

Chapter 5. The Nature of the Soil

Jesus' criticism is limited to the quantity of faith; no criticism is made of the quality of faith. An inverse relationship exists between the quantity and quality of eternal life versus that of faith.* The quality of faith refers to its purity. A faith that is purely in Christ for eternal life as a purely-free gift is saving faith. A faith that is even partially in perseverance for eternal life as a costly-fee gift is not saving faith. Since saving faith is in Christ rather than in one's performance, one unconditionally is assured of reaching heaven the moment one comes to saving faith. Otherwise, one would have to trust in one's performance to reach heaven, which is a false gospel. Once a person trusts purely in Christ for eternal life as a truly free gift, that person will always be saved: OSAS. Because the life given in response to a pure faith is an eternal gift, one gets to keep it regardless of one's subsequent performance. A pure faith results in permanent life. Whether or not the faith survives, the life given in response to it certainly will.

Persevering faith (i.e., a quantitative faith), on the other hand, is necessary for a fruitful harvest. Such faith moves beyond merely experiencing the initial life-giving properties of the life-giving seed to producing live-giving seed for others. Abundant life is the fruitful result of persevering faith. The purely-free understanding of the text is simple. Possession of the gift of life is purely-free (going on-and-on forever). The gift of life is conditioned on one's purity in faith. Reaping an abundant harvest of life, in contrast, is very costly. The crown of life is conditioned on perseverance in faith. The more faith you have, the more life you will reap.

Those in the proveitist camp, in contrast, have a terrible time with this rocky verse because here Jesus clearly affirms, in unequivocal terms, that it is quite possible purely to believe for a little while. Some costly-free advocates have combined proveitist theology with a mistaken view of God's sovereignty to pose a doctrine of *temporary faith* in which God is pictured as causing the lost to believe temporarily so that He might fool them into thinking that they are genuine believers in order that He might condemn them to hell for not continuing to believe. Even apart from such mistaken proveitist views of God's sovereignty, proveitist views of assurance are plagued by self-induced problems of their own: How can you prove you are a believer when being a believer does not prove that you are a believer? Since in proveitist theology believing does not prove that you are a believer, proveitists caution you to look to your fruits for confirmation of the fact that you are a believer. Even aside from such a mistaken view of assurance, the problem remains that the proveitist interpretation not only falsely makes perseverance in faith evidence of regeneration, proveitist theology makes perseverance **necessary** evidence so that one cannot reach heaven without

---

* See *Illustration 8. Duality of Eternal Life*, 9.

this evidence. Perseverance becomes a performance necessary for entrance into heaven. A false costly-free gospel is produced.

Some costly-free pastors have attributed the shallowness of the soil to false conversion produced by purely-free preaching. Such costly-free critics lament that shallow converts are not told about the hidden costs of getting into heaven, such as repenting from their sins, committing their lives, taking up their cross, and persevering in the faith. Naturally, purely-free preachers do not present such hidden costs because they do not perceive any such hidden costs! Purely-free preachers believe that heaven is purely-free.

The shallowness of the parabolic soil would be better attributed to the soil rather than to purely-free preachers. Granted, false preaching can produce false and shallow converts, no doubt about it. But Jesus' emphasis in this parable is not on the sower or on the seed—the preacher or the content of his sermon. Instead, Jesus' emphasis is on the soils. **Each of the soils are given the same type of seed—the same good gospel message. Thus, the faith experienced by all three latter soils is genuine. They each believe the same gospel.** Even when a true gospel message is preached and believed, however, shallow converts may be produced. Such is the message of this parable.

Tares

False converts are the tares pictured by the parable of the tares (which follows the parable of soils). False converts are not pictured by the rocky soil in the parable of the soils. Tares look and act like wheat. Costly-free legalists look and act like spiritual Christians. But tares do not produce a life-giving seed because they believe and present a performance-based gospel. Those who respond positively to the costly-free gospel are the tares. By assuming that those represented by the poorly performing rocky wheat are false converts, the costly-free claim mistakes wheat for tares. In the parable of the wheat and the tares (Mt 13:38), the wheat is identified as the *sons of the kingdom*. If it be objected that the wheat in that parable produces a crop (Mt 13:26), then let it be remembered that the parable of the soil (which precedes the parable of the tares) proves that not all wheat produces a crop. Moreover, the only other time the expression *sons of the kingdom* occurs in the Matthew (or in the NT for that matter) is in Mt 8:12, where it is *sons of the kingdom* who are thrown into the outer darkness! Not all *sons of the kingdom* are fruitful wheat; nevertheless, they are wheat, not tares.

Immature Roots

Some in the proveitist camp have made too big of a deal about the statement that the rocky soil had *no root*: "But the ones on the rock are those who, when they hear, receive the word with joy; and these have *no root*, who believe for a while and in time of temptation fall away" (Lk 8:13; NKJ). Of course, it is easier for them to maintain their mantra that root-determines-fruits if there is no root to begin with in the rocky soil. However, their shallow assessment fails to notice the shallow root.

The NAS translators correctly perceive that the text is denying any *firm* root rather than *any* root at all: "And those on the rocky soil are those who, when they hear, receive the word with joy; and these have no *firm* root; they believe for a while, and in time of temptation fall away." The parallel account in Mt 13:21 is translated similarly by the NAS: "Yet he has no *firm* root in himself, but is only temporary, and when affliction or persecution arises because of the word, immediately he falls away." The same is true for the parallel in Mk 4:17: "They have no *firm* root in themselves." (Italics by NAS in each case.)

The implication of the Greek text (as correctly perceived by the NAS) is that the plant in the rocky soil had a root, but not a *firm* root. The statement by those in the proveitist camp who say that root determines fruits is countered by the fact that the presence of a root did not determine that fruits would be produced in the rocky soil. BDAG (the standard Greek lexicon) concurs with the NAS and gives this definition for *no root* (*ouk rhiza*) in all three passages provided above: "*no firm root* and hence be easily inclined to fall away." Root was present; fruits were not.

Most translations fail to convey the implicit nature of the context by translating *ouk rhiza* simply as *no root*. If what is being denied is *root*, as opposed to *shoots* or *sprouts* (rather than *no root at all*), then perhaps a *no root* translation would be reasonable. If so, then it is up to the expositor to correctly portray the situation by acknowledging that *ouk rhiza* is a relative negation, not an absolute one. The GWN fails completely when it translates it absolutely: "They don't develop *any* roots." The word *any* is not in the Greek text. Admittedly, for that matter, neither is the word *firm*. Nevertheless, Jesus' hearers surely would be aware that for the plant to sprout up out of the ground, it first had to sprout under the ground. Therefore, the GWM misses the mark entirely. The NAS rendering of *firm roots* logically is consistent with the context.

Even so, the NLT is superior even to the NAS because NLT consistently renders both the introductory and explanatory passages regarding the rocky soil so that what is strictly denied is that the rocky soil has *deep roots* (Mt 13:6,21; Mk 4:6,17; Lk 8:13; NLT). This translation can also claim support from BDAG which defines *rhiza* in Mt 13:6 and Mk 4:6 as *(deep) root(s)*. Of course, one does not need a Greek dictionary to perceive the obvious. Aside from translations and lexicons, the context makes it clear that the seed on the rocky soil actually had sprouted and therefore produced immature roots (i.e., sprouts). For the wheat to grow up in the rocky soil (as Jesus affirms that it did), it had to have a root. The wheat could not sprout up if it did not have sprouts.

Thorny Soil

The third soil, like the second soil, is described as experiencing the life-imparting benefits of the seed: "And other seed fell among the thorns; and the thorns **grew up** *with* it, and choked it out" (Lk 8:7). The verb *grew up with* (*sumphuo*) is a compound of the verb *grew up* (*phuo*) used in the previous verse. As a result of the mutual growing, fruit production is stunted: "And the seed which fell among the thorns, these are the ones who have heard, and as they go on their way they are choked with worries and riches and pleasures of this life, and bring **no fruit to maturity**" (Lk 8:14).

Amazingly, a proveitist speaker commenting on this passage appealed to Jam 3:10-12 as a cross reference to prove that the people represented by this soil must be lost. Evidently, the intent of his appeal was to imply that since a fountain cannot send forth both fresh and bitter water and since a fig tree cannot produce olives, a genuine believer cannot produce thorns. The irrational nature of such an appeal is apparent. Believers still have the old nature within their flesh. Therefore, they are still quite capable of producing fleshly (i.e., carnal) behavior. The thorns springing forth from that old nature can quench the Spirit and severely stunt the production of spiritual fruits. Such thorns spring forth from the old nature, of course, not from the new nature. This rational conclusion is not lost on James who likewise makes this same point in the very context to which the proveitist speaker appealed. Believers can manifest carnal behavior, but this behavior comes from a demonic nature. The fruits stemming from the new nature are those of righteousness springing up from the seed that has been *sowed* (*speiro*) in the hearts of believers. (Incidentally, the same Greek word is used in the parable of the soils in which the sower *sows* the word.)

While it is true that root determines fruits in the sense that the only root and corresponding fruits produced by the word of righteousness is that of righteousness, it was false for the proveitist speaker to insinuate that such righteousness seed necessarily will produce righteousness fruits. The nature of the seed determines the scope of production, not the fact of production. The root produced by such seed (when such seed is allowed to germinate) can only produce righteous fruits, but the presence of such root does not prove that such fruits will be produced. The thorns in the thorny soil might be allowed by the individuals being represented to prevent the root from manifesting its full potential in the fruits produced. In that sense, root does not determine fruits. The soil determines what fruits, if any, will be produced by the good seed.

Christians might allow the seeds of their old nature (that still reside in their flesh) to prevent the Spirit (who imparts life to their spirits) from being fully manifested in their souls (lives). Consequently, the proveitist thesis collapses entirely. Rather than being supported by James, proveitist theology is refuted by James. Thorns *ought not* to be allowed to grow up from the believer's old nature (Jam 3:10), and such thorns *cannot* be attributed to the believer's new nature (Jam 3:12); nevertheless, thorns are found growing up from the carnal believer's old nature and spouting forth from his or her mouth. The presence of a regenerate nature does not guarantee the production of regenerate fruits. A regenerate nature (root) only makes the production of regenerate fruits possible and limits anything produced by that regenerate nature to righteous fruits consistent with that nature. The proveitist contention that the type of fruits a person produces proves whether that person is lost or saved only proves that the person making such a contention is not being consistent logically with the text.

Mature Roots

In contrast to the rocky soil (which only had immature roots), the thorny soil naturally would be understood as having mature roots. The contextual transition from the rocky soil to the thorny soil would lead one to deduce that, in contrast to the second soil, the third soil has a mature root. At the very least, even if one were to translate the rocky soil as having *no root*, then the thorny soil contrastively would have *a root*. Even if the root issue is brazenly interpreted as the complete presence or absence of root, then the third soil has a root. Just as there was a transition from *no faith* to *explicit faith* to *implicit faith* in the contrasts between the first, second, and third soils respectively, so a natural transition from (A) *no root* to (B) *implicit root* occurs in the contrasts between the (A) second soil and (B) the thorny and good soil. After all, the text does not state that the fourth soil had a root, yet the good soil certainly is understood as having a root. The same holds true for the third soil. The thorny soil had to have a root. The problem with the second soil is that it had no (mature) root. This is not the problem with the third soil. Rather, the thorny soil suffers from a different problem.

Illustration 33. Problem Progression

❶ Hard	❷ Rocky	❸ Thorny	❹ Good
No Faith	*Faith*	*Faith*	*Faith*
	No Mature Root	*Mature Root*	*Mature Root*
		No Mature Fruits	*Mature Fruits*

Dark text = Problem   *Light italic text = Not Problem*

Jesus is presenting a progression in portraying the nature of the overarching problem He is encountering regarding lack of mature fruits. The major problem with the first soil is that it has no saving faith. This problem does not exist in the remaining soils. The major problem with second soil is that it does not have a mature root. This problem does not exist in the remaining soils. The major problem with the third soil is that it has no mature fruits. This problem does not exist in the remaining soil.

Immature Fruits

Whereas Luke describes the result as producing *no fruit to maturity* (Lk 8:14), Matthew has this clarification: *It becomes unfruitful* (Mt 13:22). The presence of *becomes* (*ginomai*) in Mt 13:22 indicates that the seed in the third soil actually produced fruits before it *became* choked out.[12] The plant *became* unfruitful after initially bearing fruits, but the fruits it bore never reached maturity. The gospel accounts harmonize very well together for a joint composite. The seed in the thorny ground bore fruits, but not mature fruits. The *fruit* (*karpos*) produced by the good soil in Mt 13:8 would refer to *mature, edible fruits*. The *unfruitful* (*akarpos*) state of affairs in the thorny soil would refer to the *immature non-edible fruits*.

As already noted, Peter exhorts believers to do their best to add moral virtue to their faith so that they might achieve an abundant entrance into heaven. (See *Add Works*, 46). Such an entrance is derived by virtue of the believer's hard work in producing this godly character. Such good fruit is not experienced passively by the spiritual lazy. At the conclusion of his list of godly characteristics that are necessary for a believer to have this abundant entrance, Peter states: "For if these qualities are yours and are increasing, they render you neither useless nor *unfruitful* [*akarpos*] in the true knowledge of our Lord Jesus Christ" (2Pet 1:8). Whether a Christian is unfruitful is conditioned on the believer's performance. This word for *unfruitful* is the same word used by Jesus to describe believers who become unfruitful. Believers may become fruitful, or they may become unfruitful.

Illustration 34. Root and Fruits

❶ Hard	No Root	No Fruits
❷ Rocky	Immature Root	No Fruits
❸ Thorny	Mature Root	No Mature Fruits
❹ Good	Mature Root	Mature Fruits

The thorny soil produces fruits, but its "fruit does not mature" (Lk 8:14; ESV). In the thorny soil, life and growth are present, but no mature fruits are produced. The fact that the thorny soil bears no mature fruits does not mean that it bears no fruits to any degree whatsoever; rather, the fruits are puny and runty, scanty in amount and stunted in development.

Good Soil

Not until the good soil are all three present: life, growth, and **mature** fruits. Jesus introduces the good soil in this manner: "And other seed fell into the **good soil**, and grew up, and produced a crop a hundred times as great" (Lk 8:8). The Lord interprets it in terms of fruitful perseverance:

"And the seed in the good soil, these are the ones who have heard the word in an honest and good heart, and hold it fast, and **bear fruit with perseverance**" (Lk 8:15).

Perseverance

Proveitist apologists point out that holding fast and persevering are additional ways of describing faith. True. Of course, perseverance (in faith) portrays a positive response of faith. The fallacy comes when proveitist proponents act as though the rocky soil's receiving the word and believing the word are not equally valid pictures of faith! The rocky soil believingly received the word. The rocky soil pictures the quality of germinating faith; the good soil depicts the quantity of germinating faith. Both types of soils represent a response of saving faith. Lack of perseverance in germinating faith does not prove that germinating faith never existed!

Honest, Good, and Loyal

The great crop is not attributed simply to the seed or to the sower but to the soil. The good soil is given considerable credit for the crop produced. "And the seed in the good soil, these are the ones who have heard the word in **an honest and good heart**, and hold it fast, and bear fruit with perseverance" (Lk 8:15). The dual quality of having an *honest and good heart* is bolded in this quotation because it is in an emphatic position in the Greek text. Jesus is stressing the honest and good heart of the good soil. The *great* crop is because of the *good* soil. Just as the earlier soils are culpable for their failure to produce a crop, the last soil is praiseworthy for bearing mature and abundant fruits.

Illustration 35. The Active-Passive Rocking Horse

Some proveitist speakers like to switch back and forth, speaking out of both sides of their mouth, by saying that the fruits are produced passively by the believer and produced actively by the Spirit. They try to play down the activity of the believer and deny any merit to the believer's character or action because their proveitist theology logically conditions entrance into heaven on these fruits, and they do not want to be perceived as conditioning heaven on the fruits the believer produces or on any praiseworthy actions attributable to the believer.

Illustration 36. The Broken Active-Passive Horse

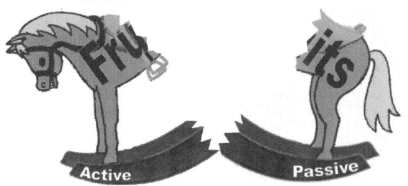

Costly-free preachers want to merit heaven without being pinned down as trying to merit heaven, so they rock back and forth feverishly trying to present a moving target. They claim that believers must bear good fruits to be saved while simultaneously attributing these good fruits to the Spirit so that the believer is denied any meaningful or praiseworthy activity in the production of the fruits. Jesus breaks the back of such a misguided perspective, however. He heaps multiple commendations upon the last soil. This soil is praised as bearing fruits because it is (1) honest, (2) good, (3) holds fast, (4) and perseveres. The fruits produced are attributed to multiple virtues possessed by this type of soil. This soil merits such approval because of its character and actions.[13]

Illustration 37. Very-Costly Preacher

Acknowledging the obvious accolades that Jesus places upon this soil poses no problem for the purely-free preacher because he proclaims that rewards are very costly. Entrance into heaven is purely-free; rewards in heaven are merited. If you want to hear the words, "Well done," then you must do well. Hearing those words of praise are conditioned on how well you do. That fact is evident from Jesus' parable of the servants. Likewise, in the parable of the soils, one must hold fast and persevere if one wants to be called *honest and good*. Heaven is free. Hearing oneself called *honest and good* in heaven by the Lord is costly.

Costly-free pastors, in stark contrast, logically end up combining the costly and free aspects, making heaven a merited reward. These forfeitist and proveitist advocates inadvertently end up teaching that good believers go to heaven, and bad believers go to hell. The outcome of heaven versus hell is not determined simply by the sower or seed in such theologies. The seed has a decisive role to play.

Indeed the sower, via the seed, indiscriminately gives the opportunity to believe. The sower, via the seed, enables each of the soils to respond positively. Yet the enablement provided by the sower does not guarantee a positive outcome. Sowing only makes fruits possible. The possible outcome is not attributed merely to the good seed, but to the character and activity of the good soil.

Illustration 38. Four Soils, Three Roots, Two Fruits, One Perseverance

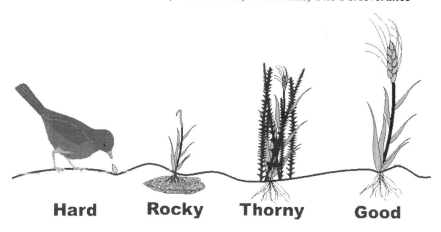

Those in the forfeitist and proveitist theologies frequently appeal to God-enabled, fruitful performance as necessary to reach heaven, claiming that they are not teaching salvation by works and are giving all glory to God. Nothing could be further from the truth. God teaches that those who try to get to heaven in this manner are trying to get into heaven by being good enough to make it to heaven. While they are pointing at the goodness of the sower and the good seed with one finger, God is pointing out that three of their own fingers logically are pointing back at themselves as trusting in themselves that they are good enough to make it to heaven because of their fruitful perseverance. Logically, they are teaching that neither faith, nor life-giving root, nor root-produced fruits are enough to make it to heaven. According to their perseverance-based theology, one does not qualify for heaven unless one perseveres to the point of producing mature fruits. God will not overlook the logical implications of their theology, even if they deny the obvious implications of their theology.

When asked, "How good do you have to be to make it to heaven?" their answer (as judged by the logical implications of their interpretation) must be, "Good enough to persevere in faith and faithfulness!" God's response will be, "That is not good enough."

In contrast to the perseverance-based (i.e., performance-based) theologies that end up logically teaching that salvation from hell is determined by fruitful perseverance, securitist theology insists that entrance into heaven is purely free. Entrance into heaven is not based on being good. Even immature believers have been born again of impressible seed so that they partake of an impressible spiritual nature and, as a result, cannot perish in hell. Even carnal (rocky and thorny) Christians have eternal security.

Rudimentary carnal security only affirms the security of those carnal believers who continue to believe. The thorny soil provides an example of such believers. Evidently, in contrast to rocky believers who only manage to *believe for a while*, thorny believers believe for the duration. They persevere in faith, but not in faithfulness. They lack the stamina to fight off the thorns and produce mature fruits. The response to the question, "How good do you have to be to make it to heaven?" cannot be watered down by proveitist to: "Good enough to persevere in faith." Not even persevering in faith is good enough to make to it to the proveitist heaven, as is proven by the thorny soil.

Making perseverance in faith a condition to reach heaven is bad enough, because even that watered-down level of proveitism is enough to drown one to death in performance-based sewage. But proveitists cannot stop merely with demanding perseverance in faith. Proveitism must progress to demanding perseverance in faithfulness and fruitfulness as additional necessities to reach heaven. The only soil to make it to proveitist heaven is the soil that perseveres sufficiently to produce an abundant harvest. Runty perseverance is not enough. The logical implication of the proveitist position is that abundant perseverance is necessary to reach heaven in the parable of the soil (and other proveitist proof texts as well). Salvation from hell by faith apart from works does not exist in proveitist theology.

Securitists reject such performance-based conditionalism and affirm that thorny believers make it to heaven even though their level of perseverance is insufficient to overcome the thorns in their lives. Moreover, securitists do not stop at merely affirming the rudimentary carnal security but acknowledge full-blown carnal security as well.

Chapter 5. The Nature of the Soil

Illustration 39. Carnal Security is Germinating Security

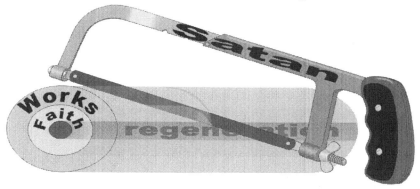

no works → no faith → has life

Naturally, conditionalists are appalled at the even more shocking, robust affirmation of unmediated carnal security advocated herein. The argument of this book is that even carnal believers who cease to believe (as represented by the rocky soil) are secure. Satan may cut through the insulating protection of their works and even through their underlying faith with his thorny hacksaw, but when his saw hits their regeneration, the teeth of his saw gnaw in vain. He cannot cut through their regeneration because regeneration consists of eternal life, and eternal life is eternal. In terms of its nature, it cannot be destroyed, not even scratched. Carnal believers, regardless of their degree or type of carnality, retain the seed of life.

The good soil represents those Christians who are not trusting in their perseverance (in either faith or faithfulness) as necessary to reach heaven. As exhorted by James, the reason they give the imperishable seed of life that imparted life to them such a warm welcome is not so that they can reach heaven but so that they can save their souls from loss of rewards by virtue of producing abundant fruits. They sink their roots down deep and successfully resist the hindrances and detractions that would otherwise prevent them from producing mature fruits. An abundant result is the outcome.

Peter describes this result as an abundant entrance into the kingdom. Paul describes it as reaping eternal life. James describes it as the salvation of the soul. Jesus describes it as abundant life and hearing the words, "Well done." Many other descriptions of this earned result are provided in Scripture as well. Since the result is earned by one's God-enabled performance, the result is a reward. Mature believers who persevere in fruitful performance will be rewarded well in contrast to those believers who fizzle out in either faith or faithfulness. Believers cannot expect an abundant harvest if they give up or produce scanty fruits.

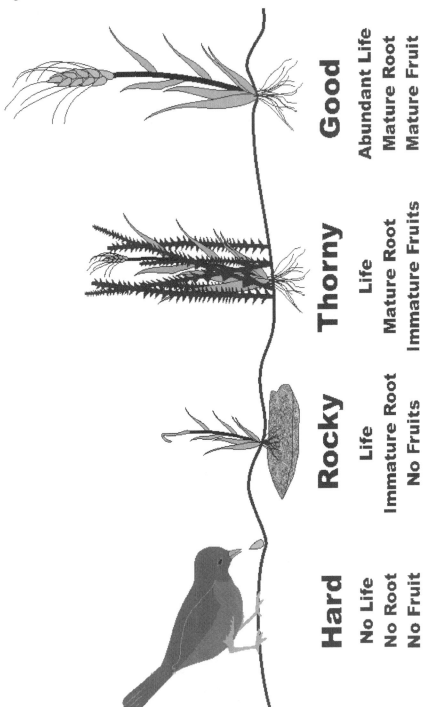

Chapter 6.
The Nature of Proveitist Evidence

Just Because

Some proveitists act as if the root of regeneration itself directly and exclusively determines destiny. The fruits of regeneration are claimed to be mere evidence of regeneration. The fruits merely prove whether or not regeneration has ever occurred. Fruits are not really necessary. When asked, "What would happen if you fail to persevere?" they would simply answer, "Such failure would prove that you never were genuinely saved to begin with." A conversation between a proveitist and a securitist might go something like this:

- Proveitist: "If you do not persevere, then you go to hell *because* you were never a genuine believer."[*]
- Securitist: "How do you know that a person who does not persevere was never a genuine believer?"
- Proveitist: "*Because* if you are a genuine believer, you persevere."

Such a proveitist is arguing in a circle.[†] In terms of how such a proveitist knows that a regenerate believer will persevere, the answer is just *because*. "How do you know that a person who does not persevere was never a genuine believer?" *Because*. No rationale is provided.

Jesus does not beat around the bush, however: "For which of you, desiring to build a tower, does not first sit down and count the cost, whether he has enough to complete it?" (Lk 14:28; ESV) If building the tower is a picture of what a believer must do to get to heaven, then counting the cost

---

[*] Note that this proveitist answer fails to admit that in proveitist theology part of the reason a person who fails to persevere goes to hell is because the person fails to persevere. Such proveitists think that fruits only prove whether or not you are saved; allegedly fruits are not necessary to be saved.

[†] In terms of logic, the proveitist merely has restated his initial statement with the logical equivalent of a contrapositive. The first statement is: If not P (perseverance), then not R (regeneration). The second statement is a contrapositive: If R (regeneration), then P (perseverance). Using negation and conditional symbols, the proveitist has only said: $(\lnot P \Rightarrow \lnot R) = (R \Rightarrow P)$. Both statements assume the point to be proven and therefore beg the question: "How do you know that a person who does not persevere was never a genuine believer?"

and building the tower are things that the believer must do in order to get to heaven.* The truth of this truism is self-evident. Proveitism makes counting the cost and paying it, in terms of building the tower, absolutely necessary to reach heaven. One does not sit around passively and trust that the tower will build itself. Even in passive proveitism, the fruits necessary to reach heaven are not produced passively. Rather, they are produced actively by the believer.

Illustration 40. Just Because

Jesus likewise says, "No one, after putting his hand to the plow and looking back, is fit for the kingdom of God" (Lk 9:62). Some proveitists bury their heads in the sand and fail to own up to the logical implications of proveitism. They pretend that someone who does not finish the building never started the building, that someone who looks back never put his hand to the plow in the first place, that someone who stops bearing fruit never bore fruit (Jn 15:6), that someone who stops believing never believed (Lk 8:12), and that the wheat that failed to produce a crop was never wheat! Such irrationalism makes this stage of proveitism completely unacceptable. Proveitists who stop here by refusing to acknowledge the necessity of the fruits in their theology are using a circular argument. Those who camp out here never make it past first base in considering the logical implications of their own theology.

When asked what would happen if a genuine believer failed to persevere, these proveitists simply refuse to go there, saying that such a

---

* Securitists believe that rewards are issues in such passages.

possibility is only hypothetical. Securitists easily can press the issue by asking, "Why is it only hypothetical?" "Just because" is not a satisfying answer. Those represented by the rocky soil *believe for a while* (Lk 8:13). What happens to them and why? If the proveitist says that this proves that they were never believers initially, then the immediate rejoinder by the securitist is, "Why? What happens to those who fail to persevere and why?"[14] Sensing the futility of stopping at this state, most proveitists move on quickly to the next stage. Proveitism logically leads to the conclusion that apostates are sent to hell because apostates fail to persevere.

Necessary Fruits

Although some proveitists try to abbreviate their conclusion, so as to pretend that *root determines destiny* in their theology, other proveitists go on to admit that a fuller acknowledgement is required: *root determines fruits, and fruits determines destiny*. The proveitist interpretation requires fruits as a necessary, intermediate link so that final salvation is conditioned on the fruits produced (cf. Mt 7:19; Lk 3:9; 13:7,9). Works are perceived by such proveitists as necessary, justifying evidence. The believer's works are considered necessary manifestations and evidences of faith. Such works do not cause a believer to become justified, of course, but in proveitist theology such works are necessary evidence of that initial justification. Final justification depends on the evidence of initial justification.

Illustration 41. Prove It!

A courtroom analogy can be used to illustrate the second stage of the proveitist argument. In the proveitist courtroom, the evidence presented by your defense attorney does not *make* (*cause*) you to be innocent, but it is *necessary* to prove that you are innocent so that the judge will declare you to be innocent. God knows whether or not you are innocent, but God will base His declaration on the evidence of that fact. Good works are necessary to obtain final salvation and escape eternal damnation. As bizarre a picture of Jesus as this may be, it is the image that logically emerges from the proveitist argument. To be sure, Jesus is presented correctly as saying, "You are saved if you are a believer." Yet He is simultaneously imagined as demanding, from proveitist lips, "Now, prove that you are a believer."

Illustration 42. No Fruits…Then No Root!

As keynote proveitists would admit, proveitist theology regards the believer guilty until proven innocent. Jesus is not only the believer's defense attorney, He is also the prosecuting attorney, demanding proof, in the form of works, that the defendant is a believer. Jesus knows whether or not the defendant is a genuine believer. But the verdict will be based on the evidence that is demonstrated before the plaintiff (Satan) and before the judge (the Father). If you cannot prove that you are a believer (based on the way you live), then you will go to hell.

The fundamental reason that proveitists think that good works are necessary indicators of whether or not a person is a genuine believer is because proveitists suppose that all genuine believers will persevere and make it to heaven as a result. Such proveitists concede that in their theology, God will not keep believers if believers do not persevere. Persevering is necessary to be kept in God's hand and out of hell. Jesus' teaching about fruit versus fire is thought to lead to the proveitist conclusion:

> [15] Beware of the false prophets, who come to you in sheep's clothing, but inwardly are ravenous wolves. [16] You will know them by their fruits. Grapes are not gathered from thorn bushes, nor figs from thistles, are they? [17] Even so, every good tree bears good fruit; but the bad tree bears bad fruit. [18] A good tree cannot produce bad fruit, nor can a bad tree produce good fruit. [19] Every tree that does not bear good fruit is cut down and thrown into the fire. [20] So then, you will know them by their fruits. (Mt 7:15-20)

Illustration 43. Fruit Determines Destiny

Contrary to those proveitists who admit that fruits are necessary but who then try to deny that the outcome is determined (in part) because of the fruits, a tree's destiny in this passage is not merely determined by the nature of the tree but also by the quality of its fruit. Although the nature of the tree might be regarded as the primary reason the tree is thrown into the fire, the fruit is the immediate cause. The bad tree is thrown into the fire because of its bad fruit.

Illustration 44. Crisscross of Tree and Fruit

Some proveitists, who acknowledge that their theology makes good fruits necessary to reach heaven, balk at the implications of their own theology at this point and refuse to proceed any further. They will admit that the fruits are necessary but try to avoid conceding that their theology pictures such people as being thrown into hell because of their bad fruits.

So they crisscross the implications of the text so as to make fruits the mere evidence of the type of tree. To be sure, it is the tree that is cast into the fire. The implication of the text is quite clear, however, that the reason a tree is cut down and thrown into the fire is because of its lack of good fruit, not merely because it is a bad tree: "Every tree that does not bear good fruit is cut down and thrown into the fire" (Mt 7:19).

Illustration 45. Just Because of the Root

Yet some conditionalists will stick their heads in the sand and try to avoid admitting that the trees (representing people) are thrown into hell or saved from hell *because* of their fruit, since in the conditionalistic mindset this would *condition* salvation from hell on works. Thus, some conditionalists act as though the fruit is necessary evidence of salvation but not a condition for salvation. After all, they equate fruits with works, and they do not want to be perceived as conditioning salvation on works.

Illustration 46. Bear or Burn

Of course, those proveitists who try to apply the brakes and stop at the second stage regarding the implications of their theology are refuted by those in their camp who proceed to the third stage by acknowledging the conditional nature of such a salvation. By pointing out the legal nature of such fruit, the fact that the verdict is based on such fruit, and the obvious implications of the text, proveitists who proceed to acknowledge that final salvation is conditioned on the production of fruit in this context win the day. Therefore, we must proceed to the next base on the conditionalistic playing field.

Conditional Fruits

The more intellectually honest proveitists face up to the logical implications of their theology sufficiently to move on to the third stage of the proveitist argument. Proveitists are conditional securitists.

Illustration 47. Performance Baseball

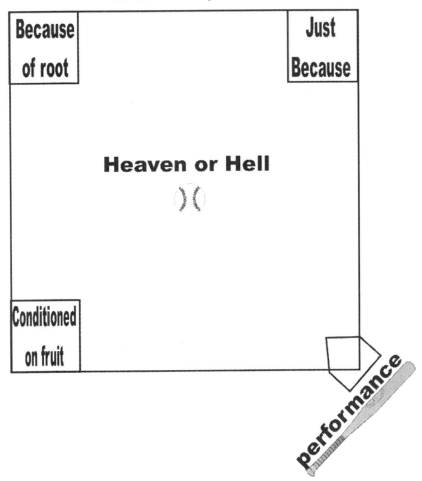

In the end, whether or not someone makes it home to heaven, gets stranded on base, or pop fouls into hell is determined by how well they swing the performance bat. If they swing the bat with sufficient strength of commitment and hit the ball accurately enough, they can make it home to conditionalistic heaven. Only the good batters are good enough to make it to such a heaven. Poor batters go to hell. Wearing a team jersey is not enough. Hitting a single, double, or triple is not enough. It is either a home run or nothing. Conditional security has no room for carnal believers in its heaven because its theology logically has no place in heaven for poor performers. *Perform well or burn in hell* would be their performance motto.

Illustration 48. Broken Faith

In conditional security, you cannot be saved by faith apart from works because you are saved by faith that works. Their argument breaks down when one tries to picture saving faith as: *faith that works* and *faith without works*. Salvation is not conditioned on any such round square.

Singular Fruit of the Spirit

Realizing that their third-base theology crassly leads to salvation by works, some conditionalists have equated this singular fruit in Mt 7:19 with the singular fruit of the Spirit. Doing so still conditions whether or not one reaches heaven on the fruit (performance) one produces. But how much fruit does a good tree have to produce to be a good tree according to Jesus in this context? Just one. The singular issue is the quality of the fruit, not the quantity of the fruit. The fruit is either good or bad. Yet not even conditional securitists believe that producing just one good deed or just one kind act or even one fruit of the Spirit on one occasion is sufficient to qualify for final justification from hell. Consequently, even by proveitist standards, something other than the fruit of the Spirit must be intended by Jesus in His reference to singular fruit in this Matthean context.

Singular Fruit of Faith

The most natural proposal is that Jesus is talking about saving faith versus non-saving faith in this particular Matthean context when He refers to singular fruit.[*] The securitist has no problem taking this passage in a

---

[*] See my *Mere Christianity and Moral Christianity* and *The Outer Darkness* for discussion of distributive plurals, collective singulars, and related contexts.

straightforward manner: Those who produce saving faith go to heaven; those who do not produce saving faith go to hell. It is that simple. Saving faith is not a performance issue. So salvation from hell is not conditioned on performance, although salvation from hell is conditioned on singular fruit.

Illustration 49. Apple of Saving Faith

Regarding heaven versus hell, Jesus' condition is that one produces a fruit that is wholly good. Partially good fruit will not cut it. The only way to produce a genuinely good fruit is if it has nothing to do with our performance.

Illustration 50. Apple of Non-Saving Faith

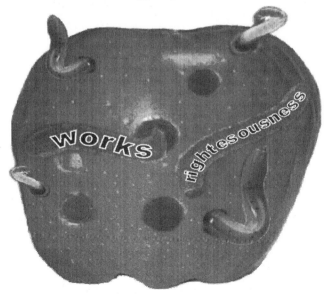

"All our righteous deeds are like a filthy garment" (Is 64:6). Our self-righteous works-righteousness stinks to God. It is purely bad fruit. To those who never produce anything but the rotten faith of works-righteousness, Jesus will say, "I never knew you; depart from Me, you who practice lawlessness" (Mt 7:23). The passage is not talking about proving your salvation by the way you live, but of failing to receive salvation because you think that the way you live has something to do with whether or not you will make it to heaven. Nor is it talking about losing your salvation because of the way you live, but of never having salvation because of what you believe.

Works count for nothing when it comes to entering heaven. Those counting the cost in terms of their performance as a condition they must meet in order to reach heaven can count on hell instead. Does this mean that works are not important? Not by a long shot. Faith without works is quite *useless* when it comes to saving a believer from a merciless judgment at the *bema* (Jam 2:20). On the other hand, faith without works is the only type of faith that can save a person from hell. Context is the key.

Jesus implicitly is describing justification by faith in this context. James, on the other hand, is talking about justification by works (Jam 2:21,24-25). Jesus is alluding to a faith that saves apart from works. James is discussing a faith that saves by means of works. Naturally, since two different types of justification and two different types of salvation are in view, one cannot equate the passages without doing serious damage to saving faith. Those who homogenize the two passages are the false teachers who produce the bad fruits of works-righteousness to which Jesus is alluding. Jesus describes such teachers in Matthew. We know they are bad teachers because of their bad teaching (i.e., plural fruits). Their faith is eaten alive by works-righteousness.

Conditionalists are false teachers because they condition salvation from eternal damnation on the rotten works of self-righteousness. Trying to pawn these works off as fruit of the Spirit or God-enabled fruit does not change that fact one iota. We need a righteousness that surpasses that of the Pharisees in order to enter the kingdom (Mt 5:19), not a righteousness that imitates the Pharisees by considering our God-enabled righteousness as good enough to get into heaven. God-enabled, legalistic performance is still legalism. God-enabled works of righteousness that are depended upon for entrance into the kingdom are still works-righteousness. Jesus is calling for justification by faith, not for justification by works, in this Matthean context.

"No singular, good fruit of justification by faith alone... then burn in hell with your self-righteous works!"

— Securitist Jesus

Chapter 7.
The Nature of Justification by Faith

Pharisee and Publican

Jesus laid the foundation for the NT doctrine of justification by faith in His parable about the Pharisee and the publican:

> And He also told this parable to certain ones who trusted in themselves that they were righteous, and viewed others with contempt: ^{10} Two men went up into the temple to pray, one a Pharisee, and the other a publican.
> - ^{11} The Pharisee stood and was praying thus to himself, "God, I thank Thee that I am not like other people: swindlers, unjust, adulterers, or even like this publican. ^{12} I fast twice a week; I pay tithes of all that I get."
> - ^{13} But the publican, standing some distance away, was even unwilling to lift up his eyes to heaven, but was beating his breast, saying, "God, be merciful to me, the sinner!"
>
> ^{14} I tell you, this man went down to his house justified rather than the other; for everyone who exalts himself shall be humbled, but he who humbles himself shall be exalted. (Lk 18:9-14)[*]

A costly-free speaker in our church correctly noted that the Pharisee would seem like the model Christian in a contemporary church. How true! The obvious point of the parable is supposed to be that we cannot be justified (in terms of getting to heaven) by trusting in our own personal righteousness or performance. This costly-free speaker completely missed this central point, however. He substituted the idea that the problem was that the Pharisee was trusting in his personal righteousnesses when he should have been trusting in God-enabled righteousness instead.

At the conclusion of the sermon, as I was walking out of the church, I asked him, "So you are saying that we should trust in our Christ-enabled performance for entrance into heaven?" He nodded his head, "Yes." Sadly, his mistaken perspective runs rampant in supposedly Christian pulpits. Tragically, he had not considered the possibility that to trust in Christ-enabled performance for justification is still to trust in one's personal

---

[*] *Tax-collector* has been changed to *publican* in this quotation to match the KJV.

performance to get to heaven. The NT emphasis that we must be justified as a gift apart from works was completely lost on this preacher. According to Jesus, one cannot be saved by trusting in God-enabled performance as a necessary means of getting to heaven.

Illustration 51. God-Enabled Performance for Heaven

Christians have been known to remark, "But for the grace of God, there go I." This sentiment is true enough. The problem is that proveitists twist this statement to mean: "But for the grace of God manifested in my personal performance, there I go on my way to hell." The manifestation of God's grace in terms of one's personal performance becomes necessary to escape hell. They believe that they are saved by the grace that enables them to work because they believe that such God-enabled works are necessary for salvation from hell.

Illustration 52. Saving-Enabling Grace

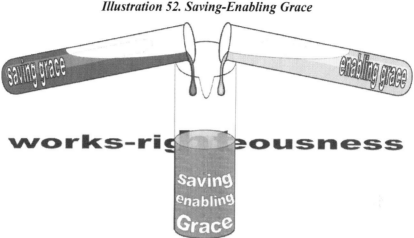

The young, costly-free speaker to whom I was listening failed to note the significance of the Pharisee's opening address to God. Much like the modern day proveitist, the Pharisee basically was praying, "But for the grace of God, there I go on my way to hell." The Pharisee opens his prayer with thanks to God for his performance: *God, thank You that I don't live like that publican.* The Pharisee attributes his righteous performance to God's enabling grace. And Jesus sentences this God-thanking Pharisee to hell. Why? Because the Pharisee is trusting in his God-enabled performance as a means for justification from eternal damnation. Jesus equates trusting in God-enabled performance for such justification with trusting in one's self that one is righteous.

Illustration 53. Saving Grace-Works

Jesus did not let the Pharisees of His day off the hook with their trusting in God-enabled performance as a means to reach heaven. Nor will Christ let modern-day Pharisees, standing behind Christian pulpits, off the hook with trusting in Christ-enabled performance as a means to such justification. This type of justification only results in the Lord's condemnation. The Bible is clear: Salvation from hell "is by grace, it is no longer on the basis of works, otherwise grace is no longer grace" (Rom 11:6).

In reality (yet unwittingly), this costly-free speaker to whom I was listening was encouraging the congregation to become modern-day Pharisees so that they too could go to heaven. As frequently happens in costly-free sermons, the example of the publican was twisted into that of a Christian Pharisee! The publican is pictured pragmatically, by such preachers, as a wannabe Pharisee. Congregants are told that believing in Jesus means committing their lives (i.e., the way they live to Christ) so that they can live Christ-enabled lives and go to heaven as result. Believing is turned into salvation by works, by costly-free preachers, even though the Bible emphatically warns that we must be saved from hell by believing that we are saved apart by works. Believing is perverted into salvation by works, which cannot produce genuine converts.

Declarative justification (i.e., being declared righteous by Christ) cannot be based on manifestative righteousness (i.e., proving you are righteous by the way you live); otherwise, the Pharisee would be the one who was justified. Jesus does not declare that those who live righteously are justified. The shocker is that He declares those who are justified have no righteousness of their own to which to appeal (God-enabled or otherwise). This publican had no work in which to believe. He could only believe in God's mercy. That was enough. He had produced the good fruit of saving faith Jesus demanded: a faith in God's goodness rather than in his own.

Any proveitist, looking at the way these men lived, would have to conclude that the Pharisee was saved and the publican was lost based on the way they lived. Judging from appearance, which is the way proveitism operates, the Pharisee had the good fruits that the publican was lacking. The Pharisee was manifesting righteousness, so the Pharisee would be declared righteous by the Lord. The shock comes when the Lord stands proveitism on its head. Yet proveitists are too blind to see it and imagine that they are being publicans when, in fact, they try to get to heaven like a Pharisee. The way you humble yourself in this context is not by attributing your self-righteous performance to God (as the Pharisee did and the proveitists do) but by refusing to trust in your God-enabled performance for justification.

Was the Pharisee wrong for attributing the goodness in his life to God? No. Even lost people are supposed to give glory to God for the good things they do and the abilities they have (Acts 12:22-23). The ability to do anything good, even relatively good (i.e., good compared to another person such as a lost publican), is attributable to God's enabling grace. Here was a man who thought he was on his way to heaven because of the fruit of godly performance he saw manifested in his life—a goodness he correctly attributed to God. Woe to modern-day Pharisees who look to the fruits of their God-enabled performance for assurance! A God-enabled performance that is contaminated with fleshly performance is powerless to please God.

Manifestative Righteousness

Nevertheless, proveitists will assume that the saved publican started living a better life than the lost Pharisee, so this proved that the publican genuinely was converted. This assumption is completely unwarranted as well. The whole proveitist notion that *if you are a genuine believer, then you will prove it by the way you live* falls by the wayside when the way some NT believers live is taken into consideration. Consider this NT believer: "But if anyone does not provide for his own, and especially for those of his household, he has denied the faith, and is *worse than an unbeliever*" (1Tim 5:8). The text does not state that such a person is an unbeliever. Rather, such a person (i.e., such a believer) is worse than an unbeliever. Also, in contrast to forfeitist theology, the NT still regards such a person as a believer. The text does not state that the person becomes an unbeliever. The whole conditionalistic schema, in which such a person is said to become an unbeliever or never was a believer, blows a flat tire on the highway of NT exegesis.

Illustration 54. Flat-Tire Believers

This NT believer did not have working faith. Most unbelievers are better workers than this believer. His dead, non-productive faith would save him from hell, but it would not save him from a merciless *bema* judgment (Jam 2:13-26) or from the outer darkness. Like the lazy slave who did nothing, this lazy Christian certainly fails to be the worker that he is supposed to be (Mt 25:26). Contrary to conditionalists, the NT regards such believers as Christian brothers:

> [11] For we hear that some among you are leading an undisciplined life, **doing no work at all**, but acting like busybodies. [12] Now such persons we command and exhort in the Lord Jesus Christ to work in quiet fashion and eat their own bread. [13] But as for you, brethren, do not grow weary of doing good. [14] And **if anyone does not obey** our instruction in this letter, take special note of that man and do not associate with him, so that he may be put to shame. [15] And yet **do not regard him as an enemy, but admonish him as a brother**. (2Thess 3:11-15)

These disobedient Christian brethren are as useless as a flat tire when it comes to putting their faith into practice. Their faith is completely dead and useless when it comes to providing for the needs of others. James does not hesitate to draw the necessary implications:

> [14] What use is it, my brethren, if a man says he has faith, but he has no works? Can that faith save him? [15] If a brother or sister is without clothing and in need of daily food, [16] and one of you says to them, "Go in peace, be warmed and be filled," and yet you do not give them what is necessary for their body, what use is that? [17] Even so faith, if it has no works, is dead, being by itself. (Jam 2:14-17)

Such believers are worse than many unbelievers. The faith of such believers is dead, useless, unproductive.[*] In the preceding verse, James warns such believers that the judgment will be merciless for them: "For judgment will be merciless to one who has shown no mercy; mercy triumphs over judgment" (Jam 2:13). Works of mercy are required in order to be shown mercy at the Judgment Seat of Christ for the simple reason that *judgment is always based on works*.[†] Christ put the relationship between

---

[*] The one holding out on *a brother* is *his brother* (1Jn 3:17-18).
[†] See *Judgment is Always Based on Works*, 121.

showing mercy to others and being shown mercy oneself (as a result of one's performance) this way: "Blessed are the merciful, for they shall receive mercy" (Mt 5:7). If you want to experience mercy at the Judgment Seat of Christ, then you better earn it by earning a living for yourself and providing for the needs of your physical family and your family of believers.

Illustration 55. Prove You are a Disciple

Admittedly, some purely-free pastors have a weak view of eternal security. Like many conditionalists, even some securitists essentially portray heaven as pie in the sky for everyone who makes it to heaven. Everyone gets a piece of the pie. Some people might get a slightly larger piece than others. But it does not matter because everyone simply will be delighted with their piece of the pie.

The Bible knows of no such pie-in-the-sky view of heaven. Jesus makes the outcome of the *bema* for Christians dependent on the proof they can offer of their discipleship, and He does not offer pie to those who do not measure up. The biblical securitist is not afraid to ask the question, "How much of a disciple are you?" and expound the negative implications that result from poor discipleship. Biblical security does not present a frail picture of Jesus' judgment. A well-balanced securitist stresses both the purely-free and very-costly aspects of eternal life. Free aspects of eternal life are free. Costly aspects are costly.

Prove It

During His earthly ministry, Jesus laid out the condition for fireproof discipleship: "If you abide in My word, then you are truly disciples of Mine" (Jn 8:31).* "He who abides in Me, and I in him, he bears **much fruit**" (Jn 15:5). "Bear **much fruit** and so *prove* [*ginomai*]" (Jn 15:8). Otherwise the believer will be cast into the fire (Jn 15:6). The only thing that is going to save a believer from being cast into this *bema* fire is fruit—and lots of it. Salvation from this fire requires fruit to the quantitative degree. The issue is not merely the quality of the fruit, but the amount of fruit. When Christians stand before the Lord at His judgment, the Lord is going to demand proof of their service (i.e., of their full-fledged discipleship). The servant thrown into the outer darkness found out the hard way that the Lord is a "hard man" to please when you have done nothing to prove your service (Mt 25:24).

The *bema* fire is going to be a scorching hot experience for those believers who cannot prove, by the amount of fruit they produced, that they were disciples. Little wonder, then, that James exhorts Christians: "*Prove yourselves doers of the word, and not merely hearers who delude themselves*" (Jam 1:22). This is a courtroom use of *ginomai*. The only way you can prove that you truly were serving the Lord during your time of earth service is by the service you performed while on earth. Your service for

---

* Discipleship is a fluid term in Scripture. In the broadest sense, a disciple is a follower of Christ, even if the follower is an unbeliever (Jn 6:60-65). Unbelievers can be pupils/followers of Christ. *Unfledged* disciples have not yet come to Christ in saving faith disciples. *Fledgling* disciples, in contrast, have come to Christ in saving faith but are not ready to step out of the closet into the arena of public confession. Secret disciples, for example, do not confess their faith in Christ out of fear of censor (Jn 12:42-43; 19:38). Naturally, believers who refuse to confess their faith in Christ publicly cannot be publically identified as Christians. In a narrower sense, *full-fledged* disciples are believers who are committed fully to following Christ's teaching (Lk 14:26-27,33; Jn 8:31). Full-fledged disciples publicly identified themselves with Christ and were called Christians as a result (Acts 11:26).

Proveitists mistakenly conclude that unwillingness publically to confess Christ proves that one is not a Christian, that is, not a believer. Passages affirming the existence of secret believers and secret disciples refute such a view. That all full-fledged disciples are Christians does not prove that all Christians are full-fledged disciples. When Christians stand before the *bema*, the Lord is not going to demand that they prove that they are believers. Rather, He is going to demand that these believers prove that they are disciples in the full sense of the word. Discipleship, in its fullest sense, is costly. Jesus will be seeking evidence that these believers have paid the price necessary for rewards. Full-fledged disciples are made—not born. More than spiritual birth is required to be a disciple in the full (normative) sense of the word.

Chapter 7. The Nature of Justification by Faith   Page 93

others is going to count big time. Did you *prove (ginomai)* to be a good neighbor? (Lk 10:36) Works of mercy are going to count a lot at that judgment.

Here is a test question pertaining to how well you are comprehending this discussion. For some people, providing the wrong answer might very well mean that they are on their way to hell. Is the grace (that has the potential to prove vain) in the following verse *saving grace* or *enabling grace*: "By the grace of God I am what I am, and His **grace** toward me did not ***prove vain*** *[ginomai]*; but I labored even more than all of them, yet not I, but the grace of God with me" (1Cor 15:10).* Is Paul saying that God's *saving grace* did not *prove vain* in his case because of his laboring service? Pause and think about that question. Proveitists are inclined to think that you are not saved if you cannot prove it by the way you live. They think that God's saving grace, drawing you to salvation, will prove to be in vain if you do not follow through in godly service. You hope in vain to be saved if you do not labor.

Hopefully, you see the futility of the proveitist answer. Such a view makes the validation of your salvation from hell conditioned on your service. A salvation that was supposed to be by grace apart from works becomes dependent upon works for its saving validity in the proveitist scheme of things. They substitute salvation by works for a salvation that was supposed to be by faith apart from works. Paul rejects such a view of saving grace: "For by grace you have been [and still are] saved through faith; and that not of yourselves, it is the gift of God; not as a result of works, that no one should boast" (Eph 2:8-9). Becoming saved and remaining saved are not a result of works. Such salvation is exclusively a result of grace apart from works. Do not add works to saving grace!

Of course, as Paul goes on to point out in the next verse, we *should* perform good works after we experience saving grace, (Eph 2:10). Why? So that we can go to heaven? No! Such a view invalidates the statement that Paul has just made about salvation by grace apart from works. Rather, as Paul goes on to explain further in this epistle, those who live immorally will

---

* This biblical view of enabling grace pictures it as working *with* (*sun*) us not *in place of* us. We are not automations or puppets that are passive in our experience of enabling grace: "By the [enabling] **grace** of God I am what I am, and His [enabling] **grace** toward me did not prove vain; but I labored even more than all of them, yet not I, but the [enabling] **grace** of God *with* me" (1Cor 15:10). Enabling grace may prove vain in terms of works we should produce if we refuse to produce them, but this would not mean that God's saving grace (from hell) proved vain because the latter dimension of God's grace is not dependent upon our works to produce its guaranteed result— salvation from hell.

not have *an inheritance in the kingdom* (Eph 5:5). And this possibility includes Christians. The believer's inheritance in the *kingship* is conditioned on his or her performance as a Christian.* Even those believers in lowly positions can qualify to become kings if they perform the necessary service: "With good will render service, as to the Lord, and not to men, knowing that whatever good thing each one does, this he will receive back from the Lord" (Eph 6:7-8). Show mercy, and you will be shown mercy. Rulership is at stake.

Mercy

"Wait just a minute!" the costly-free proveitist will exclaim, "Mercy is unearned!" This claim makes them appear, to the untrained eye, as if they champion mercy as truly free. In actuality, such costly-free advocates perpetuate the myth that mercy is always unearned so that they can conceal the works-righteousness that forms the backdrop for their view of mercy.

Regardless of the context, they take passages that condition mercy as an earned reward and combine them with passages that present mercy as an unearned free gift and think that they have discovered that mercy is a costly-free means of getting to heaven. By claiming that mercy is unearned and then turning to passages that clearly condition mercy on performance, they act as though the mercy necessary to get into heaven is an unearned benefit based on performance. Not so! A benefit based on performance is earned. Contrary to costly-free claims, a mercy based on works cannot be used to prove that the mercy necessary to enter heaven requires works.

Illustration 56. Costly-Free Mercy

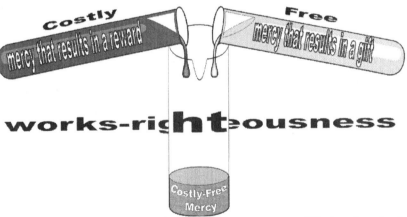

Conditionalists assume that saving mercy starts off being free (as in the case of the publican) but ends up being costly (as in the case of James'

---

*See *Kingship*, 105.

exposition). They mix costly mercy with free mercy and produce a putrid combination of costly-free mercy in their chemistry set and think that they successfully have brewed a works-righteous potion that can transform them morally into what they need to be in order to get into heaven. They have mixed nitro with glycerin to produce an explosive result that will destroy any hopes they have of reaching heaven.

Such pastors are exhorting their congregations to engage in works of mercy so that they can go to heaven as a free gift as a result of their works. News flash! A gift is not obtained as the result of one's works. You cannot go to heaven as a result of showing mercy because you cannot earn heaven. No one is going to be able to perform or persevere his or her way into heaven. The Pharisee left the temple unjustified, even though he was confident that he was justified. Likewise, many professing Christians leave church Sunday after Sunday believing that they are justified and thanking God that they have the fruits to prove it. They suppose that a convert's practical expressions of righteousness have to exceed those of the Pharisees in order for the convert to make it to heaven. So they encourage every lost publican crying out for mercy to become a practitioner of mercy so that these lost publicans can transform into Christian Pharisees and make it to heaven. This concoction only produces more Pharisaical Christians on their way to hell.[*]

---

[*] *Soft legalism*, as it is called by some proveitists, is still legalism and is quite deadly. Some proveitists simply criticize *hard legalism* (i.e., the belief that **self-produced** works play a part in final justification before God in regards to heaven versus hell). Other well-known proveitists additionally and more astutely reject *soft legalism* (i.e., the belief that **God-enabled** works provide a basis for final justification before God in regards to heaven versus hell). What is not equally well-known is that some of those who decry soft legalism are, in fact, soft legalists themselves. They are pots calling the kettle black. Such proveitists appropriately reject God-enabled works as a *basis* for final justification, but then they turn around and teach that God-enabled works are a *condition* (or *necessary evidence*) for final justification.

Instead of defining soft legalism narrowly as believing that God-enabled works provide a **basis** (or grounds) for final justification, soft legalism should be defined broadly as believing that God-enabled works are **necessary** for final justification. Whether these God-enabled works merely are evidential or are also acknowledged to be conditional is largely beside the point. Rather, the point is that soft legalists believe that God-enabled works play some type of role (whatever that role may be) in a believer's final justification before God in regards to heaven versus hell.

In stark contrast to modern-day evangelists, Jesus does not picture the publican as promising to become better so that he could make it to heaven. The publican went down to his house justified, even if he remained a publican, even if he did not try to live up to the moral example provided by the lost Pharisee. Lost Pharisees might indeed live better lives than saved publicans. The proveitist opinion that believers necessarily live better than unbelievers is patently false. Many unbelievers manifest more concern and mercy for others than do some believers. Even so, as Jesus illustrates, getting to heaven is not a matter of being better than the Joneses—or the Pharisees.

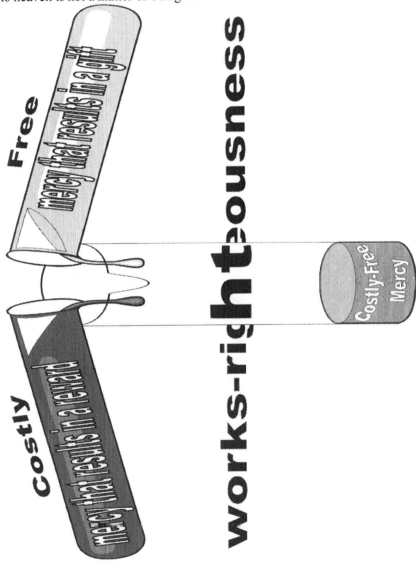

Chapter 8.
The Nature of Quality Versus Quantity

How Much Fruit

The position taken herein is that it only takes one fruit to get into heaven—saving faith. But how much saving faith must one produce in order to get into heaven? Is a singular instance of saving faith sufficient or must one produce a persevering faith? Again, the position taken herein is that a singular instance of saving faith is all that is necessary to qualify for soteric salvation. Quality of fruit, not quantity of fruit, is the issue when it comes to what is necessary for entrance into heaven.

Illustration 57. Quality and Quantity

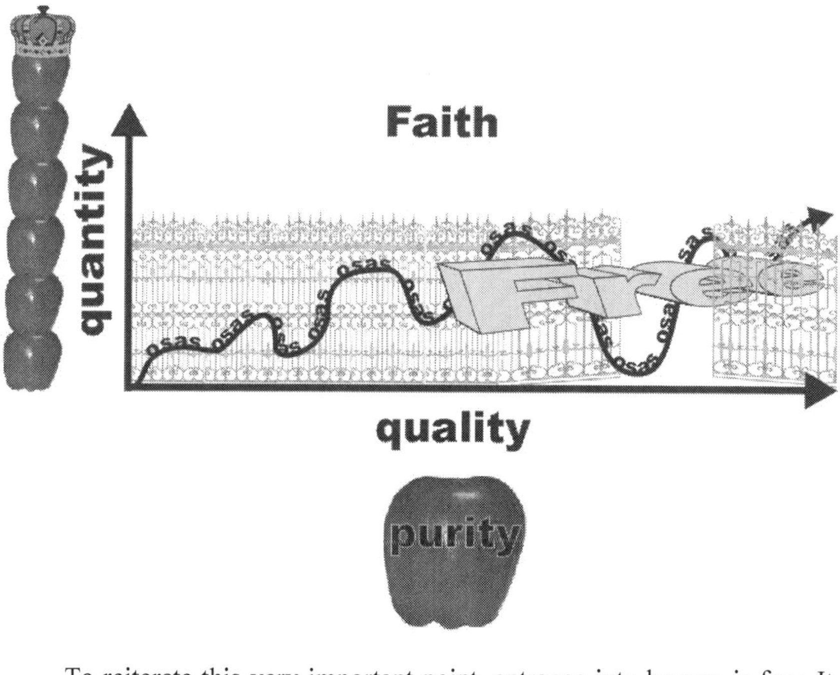

To reiterate this very important point, entrance into heaven is free. It is conditioned only on the production of one single, solitary fruit—saving faith. This particular fruit is purely passive and need only last a moment. Therefore, it is in no way meritorious. The singular issue is the purity (quality) of such faith, not how much faith one possesses. "Is one's faith exclusively in Christ alone for eternal life or is it partially in perseverance?" is the crucial question. No one can hand Christ a worm-infested apple (representing a works-righteous faith) and expect to be allowed into heaven. In Mt 7:19, Jesus is stressing the quality of fruit, not the quantity of fruit: "Every tree that does not bear good fruit is cut down and thrown into the fire." How good is your fruit? Good enough to make it into heaven? Not if it is infested with worms of works-righteousness.

An abundant entrance into heaven, in contrast, takes into consideration how much faith one has—the quantity of faith. Do you have enough faith to persevere until the end? Do not expect to live in the mansion suite if your faith gives out. Your accommodations will be in the outer darkness instead. In His very opening discussion of the outer darkness (Mt 8:12), Jesus contrasts those cast into the outer darkness with those who have "great faith" (Mt 8:10).

A little faith in a great Savior will take you all the way to heaven—if such faith is exclusively in the Savior. A great faith in the Savior and in your performance will do nothing to save you from hell. Saving faith must be in Christ alone. Still, for those who have trusted exclusively in the Christ for justification (by faith apart from works), a great faith (that manifests itself in works) is necessary for salvation from the outer darkness. The Lord is concerned about both the quality and quantity of our faith—but not for the same reason.

Jesus' Death

Anyone who has ever believed in Christ alone for eternal life as a free gift is assured of entering heaven unconditionally. Such faith has sufficient quality because it is in Christ alone for a purely-free gift. Conditional security objects that those believers who live according to the flesh will die in the sense of losing eternal life. Such a one-dimensional objection by conditional security misses the dual nature of eternal life and therefore the dual nature of death. To illustrate, consider the question: "When Jesus died for our sins on the cross, did He lose eternal life?"

Illustration 58. Did Jesus Lose Eternal Life?

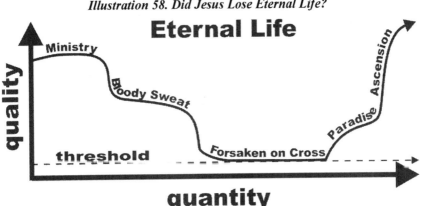

Being born in a manger was not the high point of Jesus' earthly ministry. During the course of His ministry, He would have good days and bad days, ups and downs. He was human. He was also God. As God, He also had ups and downs. His suffering on the cross was not limited to physical human pain but included the spiritual pain of taking all our sins upon Himself (Col 2:13-14). In anticipation of this event, Jesus was under such extreme distress that His sweat became bloody (Lk 22:44). That was not a good night to say the least. The next day was worse. On the cross, Jesus cried out, "My God, My God, why hast Thou forsaken Me?" (Mk 15:34) He experienced spiritual death on the cross in terms of alienation from God, His Father. Jesus' spiritual pulse flat lined. So did Jesus lose eternal life? Yes and no.

Jesus' experience of eternal life dropped just as low as it possibly could go on the cross. Even so, it could not hit zero. Therefore, on the graph, when His quality of eternal life bottomed out and flat lined during those dark hours on the cross, even at the point of His death, He still remained in possession of eternal life. His possession of eternal life did not drop below the threshold. There are some things that even God cannot do, such as cease to have eternal life.

One Christian philosopher expressed a related truth along these lines: God can do anything, not non-things. Nothing is impossible with God; non-things are impossible. God cannot die. So how is it that God died on the cross? To be sure, Jesus was God-Man. As man, He could die, pouring out His life completely. Still, it was not only as man that Jesus died, but as God without ceasing to be God.

Jesus could not die in the sense of completely losing eternal life. The basic possession of eternal life is, by its very nature, permanent. But the experience of eternal life can be like a wild rollercoaster ride, plummeting even into the depths of despair. Jesus is life, and He is the source of life for others (Jn 10:28; 14:6; 17:2; Rom 6:23). Even on the cross, He was still able to dispense eternal life to the dying thief who believed in Him, promising the thief that he would join Him in paradise that very day (Lk 23:43).

Not only did this dying thief receive eternal life from Jesus on this darkest occasion, but those who already had come into possession of eternal life by believing in Jesus did not lose it while He hung on the cross. Their source of eternal life did not dry up. He did not cease to be their source of life while He was experiencing spiritual death. Eternal life still flowed from Him to their regenerate spirits via the umbilical cord of the Holy Spirit. Even as His heart stopped thumping, He did not cease pumping eternal life to those who had believed in Him. As to the perpetual nature of eternal life, the power company, so to speak, was not destroyed nor the power lines broken. Jesus remained the source of eternal life to those who had believed in Him. They were not left running on battery power during the three-hour blackout.

Not even God quantitatively can lose eternal life, not even while bearing the sins of the entire world in His body on the cross. Unfortunately, conditionalists have the mistaken idea that our sins (such as failing to persevere in faith) can cause us to lose eternal life completely. Not so! The sins of all humanity for all time could not cause Jesus to lose eternal life completely, nor can all the sins (much less some of the sins) of a solitary believer cause the individual believer to lose eternal life quantitatively. Even if a believer ceases to believe, that believer already has been forgiven of that sin of unbelief in terms of static possession of eternal life. Possession does not fluctuate.

Similarly, Jesus did not cease to be the Son of God on the cross. His fellowship with His Father was broken; His relationship with His Father was not even strained. Believers can lose their fellowship with their Father, but their relationship with God is permanent. God still remains their God.

Some might object that Jesus fully had to lose eternal life and His relationship with God His Father in order to provide full atonement. To the contrary, He who was infinite suffered finitely so that we who are finite might not suffer infinitely. Jesus did not have to stay dead so that we could remain alive. If we finite creatures pay for our sins, then we must do so infinitely in hell. The finite must suffer infinitely, or the infinite must suffer finitely. As God, Jesus provided the latter solution—a substitution. Infinity could suffer finitely (in a finite amount of time and to a finite degree) and yet suffer infinitely. Infinity times a finite number is still infinity.

Most discussions of eternal security largely are beside the point. Loss of eternal life is discussed as if it were a one-dimensional affair. In contrast, when seen from a two-dimensional perspective, believers obviously can lose eternal life and still go to heaven. When the duality of eternal life is kept in focus, the warnings made to believers who possess eternal life make sense.[*] Paul warns believers that if they live according to the flesh, they will die (Rom 8:13). Of course, carnal believers can die prematurely and fail to experience eternal life in the form of abundant life in the here and now. More than here-and-now loss is at stake, however.[†]

The redeemed cannot die in hell, but they can die in the outer darkness in the sense of losing the crown of life (cp. Rev 3:11). In the OT, God's people died in the wilderness of unbelief and failed to come into possession of their full inheritance. They lost their hope of inheriting the Promised Land. Inheriting the land was to be a reward for fulfilling their mission successfully. The NT teaches that the same thing can happen to NT

---

[*] Believers cannot lose eternal life as gift, but they can lose it as a reward.
[†] Paul will proceed quickly to describe conditional co-glorification with Christ (Rom 8:17b). And his warning about living in the flesh in Gal 5:21 finds a parallel in Rom 8:12.

believers (Heb 3:17-4:1). There are limits as to how much believers (i.e., those who possess eternal life) can suffer, but they can suffer—even at the *bema* (1Cor 3:15).

Spiritual Suicide

One conditionalist pastor correctly noted that Christians are born in a spiritual warzone. Living rightly is an uphill fight. Unfortunately, he also said that getting to heaven is an uphill fight for the believer. Certainly not!

Illustration 59. Uphill Costly-Free Fight to Heaven

Rationally, this preacher's statement would mean that once you become a Christian, you have to fight your way to heaven. Believers have to persevere their way to heaven. In the end, heaven becomes the prize these conditionalists are fighting to win and from which they believe that they, like Paul, eventually may be disqualified:

> [23] And I do all things for the sake of the gospel, that I may become a fellow partaker of it. [24] Do you not know that those who run in a race all run, but only one receives the prize? Run in such a way that you may win. [25] And everyone who competes in the games exercises self-control in all things. They then do it to receive a perishable wreath, but we an imperishable. [26] Therefore I run in such a way, as not without aim; I box in such a way, as not beating the air; [27] but I buffet my body and make it my slave, lest possibly, after I have preached to others, I myself should be disqualified. (1Cor 9:23-27)

Heaven might have started off being free in the costly-free mentality. But getting there is a different story. Their free trip to heaven requires a lot of running on their part. This passage is so blatant in its description of conditional performance, that even some proveitists figure out that it is talking about rewards in heaven rather than about getting to heaven. Those conditionalists who have eyes to see that this passage is talking about a reward rather than a gift should follow through on the implications of such a deduction to other passages frequently used as proof texts for conditional security. One reason so many texts seem to describe conditional security is because conditional securitists have taken a multitude of texts dealing with conditional rewards and treated them as if they were talking about conditional security.

The way a believer lives determines whether or not that believer ultimately will reach heaven in conditionalistic theology. Such preachers quip: "There is no downhill ride to heaven." According to such costly-free preachers, those believers who fail to live righteously are engaging in spiritually suicidal behavior that will result in eternal suicide. Fight or die.

In the context of earning rewards, such a sermon would make sense. Unfortunately, the typical costly-free preacher is not considering receiving rewards in heaven but making a reward of heaven instead. Ironically, such preachers typically have a low view of seeking rewards in heaven. They make heaven a reward yet despise seeking heavenly rewards! Biblically, however, no dichotomy need exist between seeking God and seeking rewards, especially since those who please God by faith are those who believe "that He is a rewarder of those who seek Him" (Heb 11:6). Our God is a Rewarder!

Confirmation of Conditionalism

The principle problem with conditional security is not that it teaches that salvation is conditioned on fruit(s) but that it fails to distinguish between which aspects of salvation are conditioned on which fruit(s). Conditionalism itself is certainly biblical:

- "If you [Christians] are living according to the flesh, you must die; but if by the Spirit you [Christians] are putting to death the deeds of the body, you will live" (Rom 8:13).
- "You [Christians] are saved [by the gospel], if you hold fast the word which I preached to you" (1Cor 15:2).
- The one [who believes in Me and], who endures to the end will be saved (Mt 10:22; Mt 24:13).
- Pay close attention to yourself and to your teaching [Christian]; persevere in these things; for as you do this you will insure salvation both for yourself and for those who hear you" (1Tim 4:16).
- God will "present you [Christians] before Him holy and blameless and beyond reproach—if indeed you continue in the faith firmly established and steadfast" (Col 1:22-23).
- "Whoever [believing in Me] shall deny Me before men, I will also deny him before My Father who is in heaven" (Mt 10:33).
- "If we [Christians] deny Him, He also will deny us" (2Tim 2:12b).
- "If anyone [who believes in Me] does not abide in Me, he is thrown away as a branch, and dries up; and they gather them, and cast them into the fire, and they are burned" (Jn 15:6).
- "You have been severed from Christ, you [Christians] who are seeking to be justified by law; you have fallen from grace" (Gal 5:4).
- If any man's [Christian] work which he has built upon it remains, he shall receive a reward. If any man's [Christian] work is burned up, he shall suffer loss; but he himself shall be saved, yet so as through fire" (1Cor 3:14-15).
- "For if we [Christians] go on sinning willfully after receiving the knowledge of the truth, there no longer remains a sacrifice for sins, but a certain terrifying expectation of judgment, and the fury of a fire" (Heb 10:26-27).

Unconditional securitists fully affirm the conditional statements within the Bible, even those warnings that apply to Christians! Salvation from loss of rewards is conditional! Therefore, salvation from the outer darkness (which pictures loss of rewards) is conditional. Rewards are based on works. Consequently, salvation from loss of rewards must be based on works. Christians can fall from grace into legalism or into licentiousness.[*] The result is deadly in that falling from grace results in being cast away from Christ and being denied by Christ in terms of intimate co-ruling with Christ.

Conditional securitists cannot avoid making salvation from hell conditioned on works when they take the passages pertaining to salvation from loss of rewards and treat them as if they were describing salvation from hell. One cannot successfully combine costly salvation with free salvation to produce costly-free salvation. Rather, two different aspects of salvation must be affirmed.

Contrary to conditional security, carnal Christians are not excluded from heaven because of their performance. There is a place in heaven for carnal believers—the outer darkness. No believer is going to be able to laugh in Jesus' face and say,

> Well, it just doesn't matter that You don't think I did well. I don't care if You say, "Well done," to me or not because that is only dealing with rewards. And I don't care about rewards. I'm happy just to be here in heaven. Show me to my cottage in the corner of glory land. I'll be happy enough there that I won't care if I am not dwelling with You in Your mansion. You can have that mansion for all I care. Just give me my shack!

Contrary to the above mentality, the outer darkness is not a place where carnal believers will go laughing in Jesus' face or behind His back. They will regret their carnal decisions and lifestyle. Time will tell a different tale than that envisioned by many today who ironically are trying to earn heaven because they think that rewards in heaven do not really matter. So they mistakenly think that they have to persevere in order to get into heaven because they conclude that heaven is pretty much pie in the sky for everyone who gets there. The trick, they mistakenly believe, is simply in getting there.

---

[*] For advanced study that focuses on this concept, see *Fallen from Grace but Not from Perfection*.

Chapter 9.
The Nature of Perseverance

Persevere Your Way to Heaven

Several favorite costly-free passages speak of persevering or enduring in order to achieve some benefit or to avoid some recompense. Conditionalists make such passages conditions for reaching heaven.

Kingship

- "No one [who believes in Me], after putting his hand to the plow and looking back, is *fit for the kingship* of God" (Lk 9:62; TM).
- "Through many tribulations we [Christians] must *enter the kingship* of God" (Acts 14:22; TM)
- "We ourselves speak proudly of you among the churches of God for your perseverance and faith in the midst of all your persecutions and afflictions which you endure...so that you [Christians] may be considered *worthy of the kingship* of God, for which indeed you are suffering" (2Thess 1:4-5; TM).

Reward of Rulership

- "If we [Christians] endure, we shall also **reign** with Him" (2Tim 2:12a).
- "Therefore, do not throw away your confidence, which has a great **reward**. For you [Christians] have need of endurance, so that when you have done the will of God, you may receive what was promised. For yet in a very little while, He who is coming will come, and will not delay. (Heb 10:35-26)
- "Blessed is a man who perseveres under trial; for once he has been approved, he will receive the **crown of life**, which *the Lord* has promised to those [Christians] who love Him" (James 1:12).

Securitists understand these passages as talking about judgment in terms of being rewarded with rulership. Being *fit for* and *worthy of* the **kingdom** should be understood as being fit for and worthy of the **kingship** (*basileia*). Believers must pass through many tribulations successfully if they wish to enter into the kingship of heaven. To be fit for kingship is to be awarded rulership. Perseverance is required for rulership, not for entrance.

Illustration 60. Costly-Free Perseverance

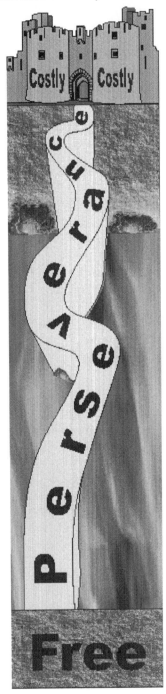

Costly-free preachers may speak as if getting to heaven is a free gift. The truth of the matter, however, is that their theology tells quite a different story. Perseverance becomes the grueling, roasting path that one must cross successfully without falling into the Lake of Fire. Those who fall from this path of perseverance will plummet into eternal death in the Lake of Fire.

Some proveitists talk as if their conditional theology portrays regeneration as causing genuine believers to persevere. Supposedly, being born again insures perseverance. Such proveitists claim that regeneration simply causes perseverance, but not out of necessity. The proof texts used by such proveitists reveal their claim to be a sham. Perseverance is biblically necessary. The real question is, "Why is perseverance necessary?" Proveitists insist on perseverance because they believe that perseverance is necessary to reach heaven.

In proveitist theology, persevering is like breathing. Yet you do not breathe just because you are alive. You also breathe in order to stay alive. If breathing were not necessary to stay alive, then you would not necessarily breathe just because you are alive. Breathe or die. Likewise, in their theology, you do not persevere simply because you are regenerate. You persevere in order that you may stay regenerate. If persevering were not necessary to stay regenerate, then you would not necessarily persevere just because you are regenerate.

Human beings breathe because they are alive and in order to stay alive. Proveitists persevere to prove that they are alive and in order to stay alive. Persevere or die in hell are the only options available in their theology.

The circular nature of the initial proveitist argument has been noted. It amounts to claiming, "If you are a genuine believer, you will persevere because you will persevere if you are a genuine believer." If perseverance is unnecessary, then the proveitist is left without rationale as to why believers necessarily will persevere.

Illustration 61. Is Perseverance Necessary?

When asked, "Will genuine believers persevere?" proveitists cannot respond, "Not necessarily." Consequently, they must explain why genuine believers will persevere—if not necessarily. They are unable to ride this rocking horse for long without breaking it.

Illustration 62. Broken Costly-Free Perseverance

Many conditionalists readily will retreat by acknowledging that perseverance is necessary. Yet some of these conditionalists will refuse to admit that this makes perseverance a condition. The reason for their reluctance is that they do not want to be perceived as conditioning reaching heaven on perseverance. Even so, their theology requires that one persevere in order to escape from the Lake of Fire. A *necessary requirement* is a *condition*. Perseverance is a condition for escaping the Lake of Fire in such theology.

Consequently, even keynote proveitists have retreated to yet another line of defense. They admit that perseverance is a condition for reaching heaven but attribute this perseverance to God-enabled performance. Despite their desperate attempts, this still makes salvation conditioned on human performance. Trying to wring the human sweat out of this perseverance-soaked theology by making perseverance passive proves equally futile and leaves one with a reeking garment of works-righteousness.

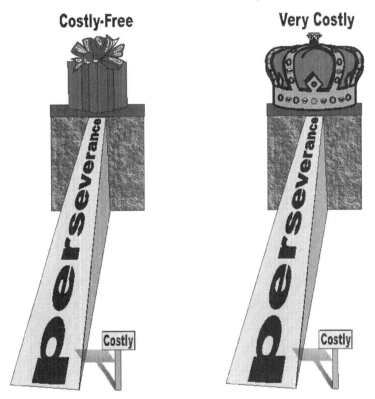

Illustration 63. Pick One and Only One

The only solution is the biblical solution pictured on the right—a solution that is eminently simple and logically consistent. Place the crown, not the gift, at the top of the perseverance mountain. Unbelievers who do otherwise will never come to know saving grace and will be cast into the Lake of Fire as a result. Believers who do otherwise will fall from grace and be cast into the outer darkness as a result.

Illustration 64. Cross-Eyed Gift and Crown

Most professing Christians will not accept eternal life as a free gift. They will add strings and conditions (under the umbrella of perseverance) to what is necessary to have this gift. The manner in which they add these requirements will vary, but the bottom line remains the same. The crown of life will be regarded as consisting of the gift of eternal life or misconstrued as the gift of eternal life so that, for all practical purposes, the gift and crown are one in the same. By looking cross-eyed at the gift and the crown in *Illustration 63*, conditionalists imagine that one is contained in the other and combine them in *Illustration 64*. They wrongly think that the gift is the crown and misperceive the gift of eternal life as awaiting them at the top of the perseverance mountain.

Purely-free pastors, in contrast, recognize the distinction between a gift and a reward and insist that since the crown of life is a reward, it cannot be a gift. Furthermore, since what is bestowed as a result of perseverance is a reward, what is bestowed as a result of perseverance cannot be a gift.

Illustration 65. Sanctified Common Sense

A little horse sense can go a long way regarding the logical implications of perseverance passages. This horse will not break. You can ride it all the way to heaven, through the outer darkness, and all the way to the throne. Perseverance is necessary to receive the stated benefit—the crown of life. Equally certain, perseverance takes a lot of work—human work. The Bible is clear that rewards are based on works. Therefore, the crown of life is a reward based on work.

A person cannot persevere in the faith unless that person first has come to faith. The crown of life is a potential reward offered to believers who persevere. It is not offered to unbelievers. One first must receive eternal life as a gift (by becoming a believer) before one can persevere and earn eternal life as a reward. The crown of life is not a reward for becoming a believer but for remaining a believer—for persevering as a believer in the things believers are called upon to perform.

The problem in costly-free theology is not that it puts costly and free items side by side but that it treats the singular aspect of some item as being both costly and free:

> [16]The Spirit Himself bears witness with our spirit that we are children of God, [17] and **if** children, then heirs also: on the one hand, heirs of God, but on the other hand, co-heirs with Christ **if** indeed we co-suffer with Him in order that we also may be co-glorified with Him. (Rom 8:14-17; TM)

Children of God are heirs of God by simple virtue of being children of God. They freely will receive the benefits that their Father freely offers them within the kingdom. Being glorified in heaven as a child of God and receiving a gloried body are free to the believer. On the other hand, not all benefits are free. Some benefits are quite costly. Co-ruling with Christ and being co-glorified with Christ as co-heirs require co-suffering with Christ. Entrance into the kingdom is free. Sitting with Christ on His throne as a co-ruler of the kingdom is not free. Just ask the apostles.

Chapter 10.
The Nature of the Danger

Implicit Is Still Deadly

Many costly-free pastors prefer to make heaven an implicit reward rather than explicit reward. Otherwise, the people in the pew would catch on more readily to what the costly-free pastors are doing and would object. As it is, their congregations are being poisoned without realizing it. Unconsciously, such congregations are allowing their pastors to plant the seed of works-righteousness in their minds and permitting it to fester into a malignant brain cancer that makes it impossible for them to think clearly enough to genuinely believe the gospel.

Congregations are led to believe that they must commit to changing their performance (and follow through on that commitment) in order to reach heaven. Consequently, even on those occasions when their pastors may spend most of a sermon stressing that eternal life is a free gift, parishioners will be hard pressed to respond savingly to the message they are hearing from their pastors because churchgoers have had the notion planted in their minds, almost subconsciously, that such a message stressing the freeness of eternal life is compatible with their belief that they must commit to living a good life (and follow through with that commitment) in order to have eternal life.

Illustration 66. I believe—But Not Really

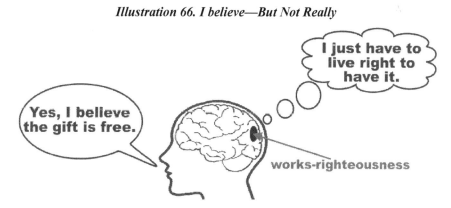

Despite their profession (and belief) that they believe eternal life is a free gift, they actually believe that they cannot have eternal life without living a good life (until the very end). In other words, they do not really believe that eternal life is a free gift; they just think they do. The worst thing about it all is that they really think that they believe that the gift is free, but they do not truly believe that it is free. The works-righteousness planted in the back of their minds makes it pragmatically impossible for them to respond in saving faith. By the frequent and predictable associations they have learned from their pastors, in connecting the possession of eternal life with a change in performance, they have been inoculated satanically from being able to respond savingly to the message that eternal life is a free gift.

Psychologists can train dogs to associate a tone with electrical shock by producing simultaneously that tone and shocking the dogs every time they feed the dogs. Eventually, the dogs unknowingly begin to associate that tone with the shock, even when no food is present. The human ability to make mental associations far exceeds that of dogs. In a similar, yet far more sophisticated manner, Satan is using pseudo-Lordship pastors to condition their congregations into associating unconsciously the free offer of eternal life with changing their performance (as a necessity for entering heaven) so that their congregations will think that they must change their performance when they are given the free offer of eternal life, even though no mention of changing their behavior is present for vast stretches of many evangelistic sermons. By rocking back and forth between saying that the free gift of eternal life is not based on performance but requires a change in performance, Satan is able to use such pastors to make congregations immune to the gospel, even on those occasions when their pastors speak correctly about the gospel. The congregation has been trained successfully, yet unknowingly (and perhaps unwittingly by such pastors), to perceive an unstated association, even on those occasions when the gospel is stated accurately, so that they believe implicitly that heaven is a reward based on their performance even when they are told explicitly that it is not. They have become accustomed to thinking of heaven as free, yet not free. Unbeknownst to them, this means that heaven is not truly free in their way of thinking.

Illustration 67. I Am Saved If...

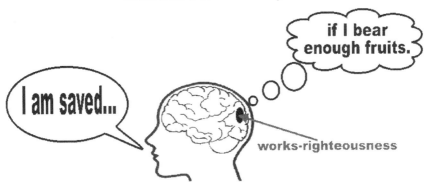

Satan demonstrated his penetrating insight into the human psyche in the Garden of Eden, and he still manifests it in typical pulpits today. He plays many pastors like a tone, using them to condition their congregations into thinking that they believe that heaven is a free gift—while unknowingly, yet simultaneously, they are led to believe that heaven is a reward. The shock will come when those who have believed this false gospel wind up in hell because they never truly believed that heaven is a free gift with no performance strings attached. Without doubt, they (and their pastors) *believe that they believe* that eternal life is a free gift. The sad reality, on the other hand, is that they do not really believe that eternal life is a free gift. In actuality, they condition their being saved on some aspect of performance, such as bearing good fruits.

Proveitists will wax as elegantly as anyone about Jesus' final victory cry on the cross: "It is finished!" (Jn 19:30) In His suffering and death on the cross, Jesus completed everything necessary for anyone who believes in Him to have eternal life and go to heaven. The payment for all sins has been made—even for the sin of unbelief. However, in order for the benefits of this payment to be made effective for an individual (so that he or she comes into actual possession of eternal life), that person must believe in Christ for the free gift of eternal life.

Illustration 68. It is Finished If…

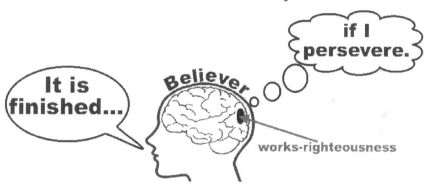

For the securitist preacher, the matter as to whether a person will go to heaven is settled once that person becomes a believer. Jesus' final statement on the cross ends with an emotional and logical exclamation mark: "It is finished!" For the costly-free preacher, on the other hand, the statement only ends with an emotional exclamation mark. In reality, they logically place an ellipsis at the end of the statement because they have an additional idea firmly planted in the back of their mind: "It is finished…if I persevere." So while they are shouting, "It is finished from the pulpit," in the back of their minds, they are whispering, "If I persevere." Logically, such a person does not really believe that the matter is finished once a person becomes a believer. They do not really believe it is finished. In all reality, they are not believers. They only think that they are. What they actually believe is that the performance requirements for their salvation from hell are unfinished.

Believing That You Believe

Many within professing Christendom *genuinely **believe that they believe*** that eternal life is a free gift. Regrettably, nevertheless, they do not *genuinely **believe*** that eternal life is a free gift—they just believe that they do.[15] Logically, if churchgoers believe that they must perform up to a certain standard in order to have eternal life, or persevere in living up to a biblical code of conduct to be saved from hell, or avoid indulging in the evil works listed in the Galatian vice list to reach heaven, then they do not genuinely believe that having eternal life is free, even though they genuinely think they do.

They believe in salvation by works but refuse to admit it—even to themselves. Costly-free advocates fool themselves into thinking that they believe entrance into heaven is truly a free gift, even while thinking that it costs them everything. Such people deceive themselves into believing that they are believers, when, in fact, they are nothing more than legalists. Over the years, I have talked to many professing Christians (and even some professing Christian cultists) who teach salvation by works. But I have never had one of them admit it. Legalists believe that they are advocating free grace when nothing could be further from the truth.

Illustration 69. Mistaken Belief

The tombstones of most costly-free practitioners could read: "He believed that he believed." Jesus said that the majority within professing Christendom would try to enter by the broad gate into heaven only to find out that they have taken a path that leads to destruction (Mt 7:13-14). In fact, one costly-free speaker read this text from a translation that presented the way to heaven as hard versus easy: "Enter by the narrow gate. For the gate is wide and the way is **easy** that leads to destruction, and those who enter by it are many. For the gate is narrow and the way is **hard** that leads to life, and those who find it are few" (ESV).

Illustration 70. Hard to Enter

The implication of the speaker's sermon was that you need to live a good life; otherwise, you will go to hell because getting into heaven is hard. Yet he claimed that he was not saying that you have to work hard to get into heaven! That particular speaker left it completely unexplained as to how his statements were not contradictory or how such statements supposedly avoided teaching salvation by works. He merely claimed that he was not teaching salvation by works and moved on to his next proof text.

Immediately after the sermon, I emailed him asking for an explanation. The bottom line is that he was taking the broad path to destruction while imagining that he was on a hard path to heaven. Trying to take the broad path of good performance to heaven is like trying to paddle up a waterfall! Most costly-free paddlers will fall to their eternal death.[16]

Jesus promises: "He who *believes* in Me has eternal life" (Jn 6:47; TM). He does not promise: "He who ***believes that he believes*** in Me has eternal life." Fooling yourself into thinking that you believe in Christ for eternal life as a free gift when, in fact, you are trusting in Christ for eternal life as a result of your performance does not qualify you as believing in Christ for eternal life. Believing in one's performance is not the same thing as believing in Christ. The only thing promised to those who trust in their performance for entrance into heaven is hell.

Control of Your Life

Many people have given Christ control of their lives earlier in their lives, yet they have faltered on that earlier commitment and have lost interest. According to some costly-free teachers, these carnal (worldly) believers have lost their salvation. Carnal believers are no longer saved in the opinion of these teachers. After all, if having eternal life is conditioned on having Christ in control of one's life, then if one ceases to have Christ in control of one's life, one loses salvation. Thus, believers who have turned away from the Lord have lost their salvation. Many costly-free advocates of the forfeitist persuasion would be satisfied by-and-large with this explanation.

Costly-free pastors from the proveitist camp contrastively would say that this type of behavior proves that such carnal believers were never genuine believers. The problem, of course, with this cop-out is that these believers did, at one time, make the very commitment regarding their performance that their costly-free pastors urged them to make, at which time their costly-free pastors promised them that they would be saved if they made this commitment. If such costly-free promises mean anything, then such a costly-free explanation is worthless. These carnal believers had made the costly-free commitment. Either that commitment does not save (and the costly-free promise is false), or the commitment does save (and salvation was lost). The promise and the perspective are mutually exclusive. Logically, one must either reject the costly-free promise or perspective—or both.

By making the question of salvation from eternal damnation revolve around who is in control of one's life, such pastors are, in effect, teaching a revolving-door salvation: Salvation becomes an on-again-off-again experience. If Christ must be Lord of your life in order for you to be saved (and if Christ must be Lord of all to be Lord at all—another popular costly-free sentiment), then not only are such pastors teaching salvation by works, they are teaching a revolving door salvation by works. When your performance is not up to snuff, then you are not doing enough to be saved. After all, according to such pastors, you cannot have self on the throne of your life and expect Jesus to save you. The logical outcome of such theology is that you would have to keep Jesus on the throne of your life/performance, in order to stay saved.

Unconditional security, in contrast, teaches that eternal life is eternal life, not temporary life: A life that is eternal cannot be lost, and a gift cannot be earned. Granted, one reason many fizzle in their commitment to the Lord is because they were never really saved in the beginning. They merely believed that they believed. They were never genuine believers. From the onset, they bought into the costly-free lies that their salvation was a free gift apart from works that was conditioned on their works.[17] The mental strain of this irrationalism takes its toll on the intellect, making it difficult for logically consistent people to maintain. Perhaps the reason some fizzle is because they just got tired of trying to earn heaven by their performance while being told that heaven is a free gift. They simply may have tired of the irrationalism inherent in the evangelistic messages they have heard all their lives. Maybe they became disillusioned with the illusion of costly-free salvation. Having heard nothing but irrational explanations, they may not realize that an alternative is possible.

On the other hand, the commitment of a genuine believer also may fizzle out. Being a genuine believer does not make one immune to the fizzle. Eventually, even genuine believers might buy into the legalistic perspective being touted by many (so-called) Christians and come to view their performance as necessary to reach heaven. If so, these genuine believers will become hamsters running around in never-ending circles trying to escape hell.* Satan is firing fiery darts; he is not shooting blanks. The battle for the believer's mind is real, and some believers do not win that battle. After all, why would Satan keep aiming fiery darts at the minds of believers if these darts were not able to find their mark? And why would believers be encouraged to wear a helmet of salvation if their minds were not susceptible to being deceived? Even genuine Christians within the Bible have been known to leave their first love for the Lord (Rev 2:4). Why? Because they have failed to remember what is at stake. This is why the biblical solution to carnality is, "Remember" (Rev 2:5).

Those who were never saved to start with (because they thought that their salvation from hell was contingent on their performance) need to be shown that eternal life is a free gift. They need to be awakened to the genuine freeness of God's saving grace by realizing that it is not conditioned on their performance, despite the numerous sermons they have heard to the contrary all their lives.

Genuine believers will need to remember what is at stake: salvation from *the outer darkness*, that is, from loss of rewards in heaven (not to mention painful experiences on earth from the discipline of their Father). They should not let licentious friends cause them to forget what is at stake:

---

* Linear running for the prize/reward of eternal life is biblical. In such running, one is not running for the gift of eternal life which one already possesses. The gift is free to keep. One is running for a fuller dimension of eternal life than one would be freely entitled. *Free ☼ costly* running around in circles, on the other hand, for the gift of eternal life is not biblical. In terms of *Illustration 71*, the gift of eternal life which qualifies one to enter the kingdom cannot be lost. That dimension of eternal life is nonforfeitable. However, the here-and-now experiential dimension of eternal life (namely abundant life) and the reward form of eternal life (such as the crown of life) are indeed forfeitable.

Christians are loved conditionally in regards to being a servant of Christ and are subject to the outer darkness if they fail in their service.

Believers also will need to remember what is not at stake: unconditional security from the flames of hell. Genuine believers will be tempted by legalistic friends who try to combat licentiousness by threatening hell on ungodly performance (and thereby conditioning heaven on godly performance). These legalistic friends mean well. But their antidote is deadly. It will send false believers to hell and can even result in genuine believers spending eternity in the outer darkness if they adopt this legalistic mindset. Genuine believers should not let their legalistic friends cause them to forget what is not at sake. Christians are loved unconditionally as children of God and never can be subject to the flames of hell.

Illustration 71. Three Types of People

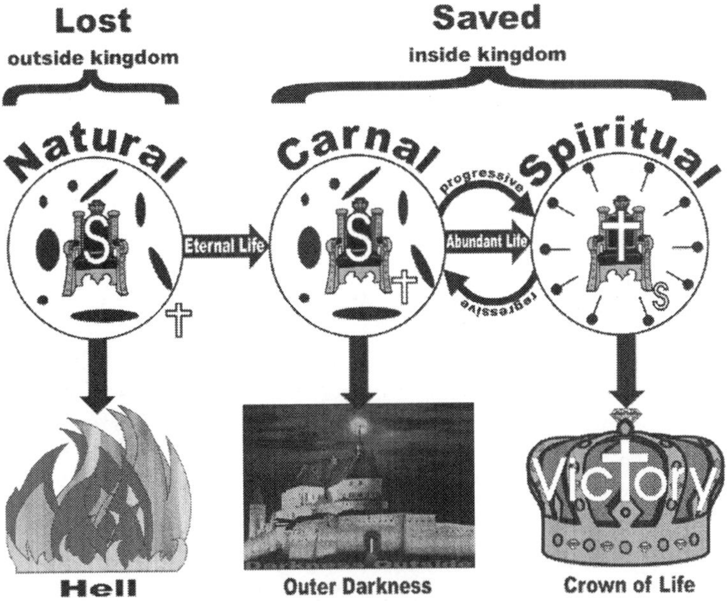

Christ (represented by the cross in the above illustration) does not reside within those people who are in their natural state. Naturally, they have *self* (represented by the large *S*) on the throne of their lives. Those who die in this state of not having Christ in their lives will go to hell because they do not have eternal life. The issue is not who is in control of their lives. When it comes to heaven versus hell, the only question is, "Do you have eternal life?"*

---

* Receiving the free gift of eternal life is a one-way trip. One cannot go to hell once one has received eternal life because this life is truly free and eternal. By

Chapter 10. The Nature of the Danger

Those who receive eternal life (by believing in Jesus for eternal life) start off the Christian life as immature believers at the point of new birth. This stage cannot be bypassed. One is born as a baby, not as an adult. Full-fledged disciples are made, not born. As newborn believers, they are on the throne of their lives even though Christ is in their lives and has given them eternal life. Realistically, the costly-free demand that people receive eternal life by bypassing the infant stage and making Christ Lord of their lives is a demand for the impossible. Skipping the immature stage of fleshly self-centeredness is impossible. Trying to skip it is deadly. Those who skip over the reality of carnality land in legalism.

If immature believers persist in this carnal state—doing nothing for the Lord and not developing a Christian character—they will be subjected to the outer darkness. Being cast into the outer darkness is pictured by Scripture as being cast outside the king's palace, not outside the king's kingdom. This darkness represents loss of rewards in heaven (and all that entails). No one who is subjected to the outer darkness will laugh in the Lord's face and say that living for the Lord really did not matter. Unfaithful believers will weep when the full realization of what they have lost comes crashing down upon them. They will live with King Jesus in His kingdom, not rule with King Jesus from His capital city. Of course, this kingdom will have many cities. All kingdoms do, and this kingdom is no exception. The Lord puts His faithful believers in charge of these cities (Lk 19:17-19). Unfaithful believers may live in them, but they will not rule them.

Those believers who progress to spiritual maturity can expect to experience the fruit of the Spirit now and reap abundant life in terms of kingdom rulership in the future.* Life now will not be easy necessarily, but faithful believers will reap eternal life in the form of the crown of life as a result of their Spirit-enabled faithfulness and fruitfulness. They, and they alone, will hear the words, "Well done, good and faithful slave; you were faithful with a few things, I will put you in charge of many things; enter into the joy of your master." Hearing these words is conditioned on how well believers do and thus on their performance. These words are not a gift. They are costly, indeed, very costly. Compared to the benefit bestowed, the cost is

---

the sheer nature of the case, a life that is possessed already and that is eternal cannot be lost.

* Moving to Christian maturity is not a one-way trip. The course is hard; the race is long; the obstacles are many; the temptations are real; the counterfeits are hard to discern, and the opponents are fierce. Failure is possible. Progression in sanctification is not guaranteed, and regression in practical sanctification is possible. One may lapse back into a carnal state; one might even stay there. Fleshly indulgence is not the only way to fall back into carnality. Legality is a sure-fire means of falling from grace into fleshly performance as well.

practically inconsequential, yet not completely inconsequential. The Bible tells us to count the cost, not ignore it.

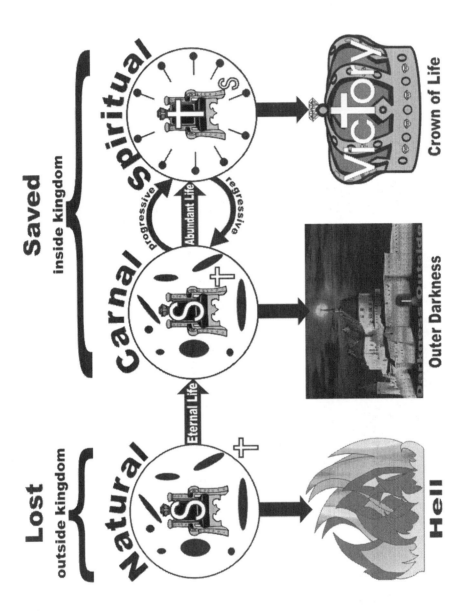

Appendix 1.
Judgment is Always Based on Works

Judged For Works

The Bible frequently affirms that judgment is *according to* works.* This association is apparent even on those occasions in which it is not stated explicitly. In the parable of the sheep and the goats, for example, Jesus states that the sheep inherit the kingdom because of their performance: "Inherit the kingdom...*for* I was hungry, and you gave Me something to eat" (Mt 25:34-35). The word *for* provides the *reason* the sheep inherit the kingdom. One of the most well-known verses in the Bible pertaining to judgment expresses the synonymous relationship between *for* and *according to* this way: "For we must all appear before the judgment seat of Christ, that each one may be recompensed *for* his deeds in the body, *according to* what he has done, whether good or bad" (2Cor 5:10). To be judged or rewarded *for* your works is to be judged or rewarded *according to* your works.†

---

* On numerous occasions, the Greek text explicitly states that judgment is *according to* works (Ps 28:4; 62:11; Prov 24:12; Is 59:18; Jer 17:10; 25:14; 32:19; 50:29; Lam 3:64; Eze 24:14; 36:19; Hos 12:2; Mt 16:27; Rom 2:6; 11:15; 2Cor 5:10, 2Tim 4:14; 1Pet 1:17; Rev 2:23; 18:6; 20:12-13). The purpose of judgment is to dispense rewards, not to hand out gifts. Rewards are always based on works (Ruth 2:12; 2Chron 15:7; Jer 31:16; 1Cor 3:14). The Lord positively repays/rewards righteous works (1Sam 26:23; 2Sam 22:21,25; Ps 18:20,24). Note righteous works are not works of self-righteousness when works are performed by the righteous to earn rewards rather than in a vain attempt to earn a gift. Judgment day is payday, not gift day. Contrary to the CSB, and as noted by practically every other translation of Is 40:10, rewards are synonymous with recompense—not with gifts! "The Lord God will come with might, with His arm ruling for Him. Behold, His *reward* is with Him, and His *recompense* before Him." The CSB correctly associates reward with recompense in Is 62:11. Repayment/recompense is based on works (2Sam 3:39; Job 34:11; Ps 28:4; 62:12; Is 59:18; Jer 16:18; 25:14; 50:29; 51:24; Lam 3:64; Eze 7:9; Hos 4:9; 12:2; Mt 6:4,18; Mt 16:27; Lk 14:14; 2Tim 4:14; Heb 10:30; Rev 18:6; 22:12). Obviously, in view of numerous texts affirming that God repays good for good and evil for evil, isolated verses like Job 41:11 and Rom 11:35 should not be twisted to mean that God does not repay those who serve Him. Rather, we have never given first to the Lord so as to obligate Him to repay us. The Lord takes the initiative, with His promises to us, in obligating Himself to reward us. We cannot take the initiative in obligating God to reward us by our service to Him.

† BBE, ESV, NIV, NLT, NRS use *for* in place of *according to* in Rev 18:6.

Judged By Works

The Great White Throne Judgment figures prominently in discussions of rewards and implements a synonymous parallelism. As seen in the manner in which various translations handle this verse, *according to* may also be used interchangeably with *by*: "The dead were judged *by* [*ek*] what was written in the books, *according to* [*kata*] what they had done" (ESV; cp. NET). Conversely, "the dead were judged *according to* their deeds, *by* what was written in the scrolls" (NAB; cp. NKJ). Alternatively, both expressions might be rendered as *by*: "The dead were judged *by* what was written in the books, *by* what they had done" (RSV).

Judged on the Basis of Works

Or one might translate the synonymous expressions used of the Great White Throne Judgment as *basis of* and *based on*: "The dead were judged on the *basis of* what they had done, as recorded in the books. The sea gave up its dead. Death and hell gave up their dead. People were judged *based on* what they had done" (Rev 20:12-13; GWN). As seen in this passage, judgment is *ek/kata* works. Making a sharp distinction between the two terms would be ill-advised. People are judged *by/on the basis of/based on/according to* their works.

False Dichotomy

A judgment *according to* works is a judgment *based on* works. Nevertheless, some proveitists make a sharp distinction between *basis (ek)* and *according to (kata)* so as to claim that salvation from hell is *according to* works but not *based on* or *by* works. The biblical distinction between *according to* and *basis* regarding this issue, however, is not nearly as sharp as some proveitists make it out to be.[18]

This ridged proveitist distinction poses a false dichotomy in that the English phrase *on the basis of* appropriately renders the courtroom setting. The verdict in a courtroom is rendered *on the basis of* the evidence. Judgment is passed *based on* the evidence. The proveitist attempt to make a sharp distinction between basis as *grounds* versus basis as *evidence* is nothing more than a futile attempt to hide the fact that such proveitists are teaching salvation *by* works when they make salvation from hell *according to* works. Judgment always is *based* on works as the *necessary evidence* for the verdict. A salvation granted as a result of such judgment would be *by* works.[19]

Judged from the Book of Works

As noted by many, judgment is always according to works. As demonstrated herein, a judgment *according to* works is a judgment *based on* works. Salvation from hell is not determined by works, however. The passage regarding the Great White Throne Judgment vividly expresses this truth:

> ¹² And I saw the dead, the great and the small, standing before the throne, and **books** were opened [i.e., Books of Works]; and another **book** was opened, which is the **Book of Life**; and the dead were judged from the things which were written in the **books** [i.e., Books of Works], according to their deeds. ¹³ And the sea gave up the dead which were in it, and death and Hades gave up the dead which were in them; and they were judged, every one of them according to their deeds. ¹⁴ And death and Hades were thrown into the lake of fire. This is the second death, the lake of fire. ¹⁵ And if anyone's name was not found written in the **Book of Life**, he was thrown into the lake of fire. (Rev 20:12-15)

Illustration 72. Two Sets of Books

Two classes of books are observed readily in this passage. The Book of Life is in a class all by itself and thus is pictured as being in a bookcase all by itself in the above illustration. The judgment is not based on what is written in the Book of Life. Judgment, as always, is based on works. Specifically, those being judged are judged *from the things which were written in the **books*** (i.e., Books of Works). They are not judged from what is written in the Book of Life.

Jesus promises, "Truly, truly, I say to you, he who hears My word, and believes Him who sent Me, has eternal life, and does not come into judgment, but has passed out of death into life" (Jn 5:24). One is not judged to determine if one has eternal life. There is no such judgment. Judgment is always based on works, not on whether one has eternal life. The possession of eternal life is an open-and-shut case (pictured by a separate bookcase). Open the Book of Life, and see if your name is written there. Those who understand and believe the full significance of Jn 5:24 can open the Book of Life even now, by faith, and see their names written there. They do not need to wait for judgment day to know whether or not their names are there.

In harmony with Jesus' assurance in Jn 5:24, this passage regarding the Great White Throne Judgment assures us that the possession of eternal life is a different matter altogether—not a judgment according to works. For believers, judgment according to works is for the purpose of determining their degree of life, not for determining their possession of life. For unbelievers, judgment according to works is for the purpose of determining their degree of death, not for determining their possession of life. Hell will not be equally hot for all unbelievers. Conversely, heaven will not be equally pleasant for all believers. Each set will be judged, at their respective times, according to their works, to determine what degree of reward or punishment will be meted out to them individually.

Appendix 2.
Enochian Darkness

As to the historical background for the *outer darkness* in Matthew's gospel, some have made a big deal out of the way the *darkness* is used in the books of Enoch and equated the two. Indeed, Jesus' palace parable about the outer darkness may indeed reach back to Enoch for the imagery. In Jesus' second passage on the outer darkness, it is pictured as being cast outside of a wedding feast that a king gave for his son that took place at night.

> [11] But when the king came in to look over the dinner guests, he saw there a man not dressed in wedding clothes, [12] and he said to him, "Friend, how did you come in here without wedding clothes?" And he was speechless. [13] Then the king said to the servants, "Bind him hand and foot, and cast him into the outer darkness; in that place there shall be weeping and gnashing of teeth." (Mt 22:11-13)

Similarly, according to the Enochian writings,

> when the last [righteous] one arrives, he [the Lord] will **bring out** Adam, together with the ancestors; and he will **bring** them **in** there…just as a person invites his best friends to have dinner with him…and they talk together **in front of that man's palace**, waiting with joyful anticipation to have dinner. (2En 42:5)

The parallels are striking. At the consummation of this age, there will be an eschatological dinner in paradise to which all of God's friends are invited. It is compared to a king's palace, where they stand outside anticipating the feast inside. It is very easy to picture this as the background for Jesus' parable in Mt 22:14. All those who are truly the king's friends will come to the palace inside the kingdom (the kingdom representing paradise) to participate in the feast.

In contrast to the works-righteousness writings of Enoch, however, the Lord gives a surprising ending. Those who are not ethically worthy to participate in the feast will be brought out (cast out) of the feast. To go outside and to be outside of the banquet do not mean to go out of paradise or to be outside of paradise; it simply means to go out of the palace (i.e., to be outside in front of the palace but still in paradise). Therefore, if some of the king's friends are cast out of the palace, it should be taken to mean that they are removed out of the feast through the front door of the palace, not out of the kingdom.

Illustration 73. Darkness Outside the King's Palace

The Lord gives a shock to the stock Enochian backdrop. Jesus counters the works-righteousness associated with the darkness in the Enochian material by disassociating the darkness outside the palace with the fires of hell. After all, even in Enochian material, one cannot equate being outside the palace with being in the Enochian fire! Moreover, if this dinner is understood as taking place at night (a reasonable presumption), then those standing outside the palace waiting for dinner are standing in the darkness outside the palace—in joyful anticipation of the dinner to be eaten inside—even in the Enochian writings! The fuller online context reads as follows:

> And I saw the key-holders and the guards of the **gates of hell** standing, as large as serpents, with their faces like lamps that have been extinguished, and their eyes aflame, and their teeth naked down to their breasts. And I said to their faces, "It would have been better if I had not seen you, nor heard about your activities, nor that any member of my tribe had been brought to you. To what a small extent they have sinned in this life, but in the eternal life they will suffer forever."
>
> And I **ascended to** the east, into the **paradise** of Edem, where rest is prepared for the righteous. And it is open as far as the 3rd heaven; but it is closed off from this world. And the guards are appointed at the **very large gates** of the east of the sun, angels of flame, singing victory songs, never silent, rejoicing at the arrival of the righteous. When the last one arrives, he will **bring out** Adam, together with the ancestors;

and he will bring them in there, so that they may be filled with joy; just as a person invites his best friends to have dinner with him and they arrive with joy, and they talk together **in front of that man's palace**, waiting with joyful anticipation to have dinner with delightful enjoyments and riches that cannot be measured, and joy and happiness in eternal light and life (2En 42:1-5)[20]

Two different sets of gates are present in this Enochian text: one gate for hell and another gate for paradise. Enoch ascends from the gates of hell to the gates of paradise. The gates of paradise are closed off from the gates of hell and separated by his lengthy ascension. Enoch pictures the place outside the palace to be a place of joyful anticipation of the dinner. Logically, to be cast back into this place after the dinner has started (which is the case in Matthew's gospel) would not picture being cast into fire. Those in this place outside the front of the palace before the dinner were not in fire, and those in this identical place after dinner are not in fire. The darkness outside the front of the palace is not a place of fire.

With a stroke of genius, Jesus adds *the outer darkness* as a buffer zone between the outside of the palace and the darkness of hell. What Enoch left open to question, Jesus settles beyond question: This buffer zone is inside of paradise, far removed from the gates of hell. To be in the darkness outside the palace is to be within the gates of paradise. To get to the Enochian hell, one would have to stroll across the dark grounds outside the palace, exit the gates of paradise, descend back down to the realm of hell, and enter the gates of hell. None of these things happens to those cast into the Matthean outer darkness. Being cast into the biblical outer darkness is to be cast outside of the king's palace, not outside of the king's kingdom. In contrast to the Enochian writings, the darkness outside the palace is not to be equated with the flames of hell but with being outside the palace—as even unwittingly allowed by Enochian writings!

Enochian material cannot be credited with perceiving that the darkness outside the Enochian palace would not be equated with the darkness inside the Enochian hell. The Enochian material is blind to the deficiency of its own imagery. The genius displayed by Matthew's writings (in picking up on the Enochian discrepancy between the darkness in hell versus the darkness outside the palace) must be attributed to Jesus Himself.

In placing unfaithful believers in the darkness outside the palace rather than in the darkness of hell, Jesus towers above the works-righteousness found in Enochian writings. Those costly-free interpreters who try to reduce the outer darkness to the darkness of hell are robbing Jesus of the credit He rightfully deserves for rejecting works-righteousness with His treatment of the outer darkness. Jesus purposefully places those in the outer darkness within paradise. At most, Enochian material does so accidently.

Illustration 74. The Darkness Outside is Inside the Gates of Paradise

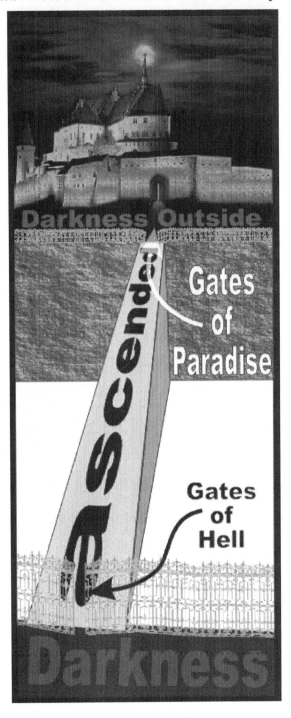

Endnotes

[1] Apparently, it escapes the notice of the costly-free group that Lucifer was kicked out of heaven because he wanted more than just to be in heaven. He wanted to rule the place. The very thing that Lucifer wanted is offered to believers who are willing to pay the price. Lucifer risked everything in disobeying God in a vain attempt to become an exalted ruler. Christians must risk everything in obeying God in order to become exalted rulers. Merely being in heaven is not what the spiritual warfare is all about. Christians are offered the possibility of sitting with the Lord Himself on His throne ruling the universe. For rebuttal of the costly-free perspective that one cannot *live like the devil* and still go to heaven, see *Woolly Wolves and Woolless Sheep*.

[2] Legalism is viewing any good work you perform as a requirement to enter heaven. Trusting what Christ is doing through you (in the way you live) rather than exclusively in what Christ has done for you (in giving you eternal life as a free gift) is a popular form of legalism. Many legalists fool themselves into thinking that they are not trusting in their fleshly performance when they trust in their God-enabled performance for entrance into heaven. They think it is okay to trust in their performance as a condition for reaching heaven as long as they view that performance as God-enabled. However, God-enabled works are still works. And God warns that He will not save us on the basis of our works, only on the basis of our faith. God-enabled legalism is still legalism, and it leads to hell.

[3] The parable of the laborers in the vineyard does not form an exception to the expectation that those believers who have been in the Lord's service for many years would be expected to have produced more return than those who had only been believers for several days (Mt 20:1-16). Those who worked all day were expected to perform a day's worth of work. Those who worked only one hour were not expected to produce as much as those who worked all day. The reason those who worked less were rewarded as much is not because they produced as much. Rather, because they believed more in the gracious nature of the rewarder, they were rewarded as much congruently as those who served contractually.

Whereas the other parables mentioned in the body of the present text show God rewarding believers according to their identity, ability, and maturity in Christ, the parable of the laborers shows Him rewarding them according to their *opportunity*. In this respect, God is an equal opportunity employer. All believers have an opportunity to be kingdom rulers. Yet as seen in parables that go into greater detail on that particular aspect of the reward, not all believers will rule equally.

⁴ Even if this position concerning the time is not accepted, the unworthy slave could still represent a genuine believer just as the foolish virgins do in the previous parable.

⁵ If it is objected that since spiritual gifts are forfeitable, so the gift of eternal life must be forfeitable also, let it be remembered that spiritual gifts are not necessarily eternal (1Cor 13:8-10). The spiritual gift is not taken away before it has run its allotted course. The reward is having the gift extended beyond its freely allotted time. For example, it is one thing for a firm to give an employee a car to use freely for an entire year. It is quite another for the firm to transfer possession of that car over to the employee at the end of the year because of his or her exceptional service. The usage for a year might be considered a perk (perhaps even a gift); ownership would be considered a reward, not a right for simply being an employee.

A spiritual *gift*, as such, is a God-given energization for service during the allotted time in which that gift is intended to be used freely in performing that service. Apparently, even those who had the gift of tongues, for example, lost the exercise of that gift within the course of their lifetime because the gift was not intended to run the course of their lifetime. The gift was expected to be in operation during their lifetime, not throughout their lifetime. What was freely given was the ability to exercise this gift for a limited period of time, not for an unlimited period of time.

Spiritual gifts cease to be gifts that may be used freely once they have run their intended course. Even the gift of teaching will cease once a Christian teacher dies or is raptured because the capacity to use this gift freely was limited to his or her time on earth during the present advent. Whether or not that capacity to teach is granted again in heaven will be contingent upon one's service on earth. If one has been a faithful teacher on earth, then one will be rewarded with increased ability and opportunity to teach in heaven. The talent that was given freely to be exercised on earth will be increased for exercise in heaven—if the believer has been faithful in the exercise of that talent on earth. Otherwise, that talent will be taken away and given to someone else.

It is not the spiritual *gift*, as such, that is taken away since the stage of that capacity to serve as a *gift* will have ceased already. Rather, what is taken away and given to another as a reward is the capacity to perform that function (that was previously a gift but that has now become a reward). As to tongues, presumably there will be no need of this gift in heaven in order to talk to men or angels. What about needing it to talk to animals? Even if some animals are able to talk in heaven, it is unreasonable to think that all animals will be able to speak with equal clarity. Some animals may need an interpreter. Believers who have been faithful in their exercise of the gift of tongues or interpretation during their lifetimes on earth may find in the new earth that they are able to talk to the animals with whom no one else is able to talk. Could it be that the stars actually sing and the creation literally groans (Job 38:7; Rom 8:21). Perhaps, these believers will be able to commune with nature at a level no one else can fathom.

[6] The casting of the saved servant into the outer darkness does not disprove eternal security. In Jn 15:6, Jesus says that He will cast some believers out, but in that same gospel He also says that He will never cast any believer out (Jn 6:37). The point is that as a believer you will never be cast out in terms of relationship, but you can be cast out in terms of fellowship. Believers may be cast out in terms of communion, not in regards to union. This Matthean parable demonstrates so well what Paul stated so emphatically in Eph 2:8—you are saved by grace. The unworthy slave did not serve his master, but his life was still spared. If entering into joy or being cast into the outer darkness in Mt 25:14-30 refers to salvation from hell, then salvation from hell is by works. But such cannot be the case and is not the case.

The most surprising thing about the parable of the talents is not that some Christians are pictured metaphorically as being cast into the outer darkness. Rather, the surprise comes from noting to which Christian this happens. The Christian in the greatest danger in this parable is not the ten-talent or five-talent Christian but the one-talent Christian. Normally, the Christians who do not have as much ability are the ones who sit back and let others do the work. They say, "Let the pastor do it." "Let those who are already deacons do it." "Let so-and-so keep teaching; I want to sit back and enjoy hearing the lesson." They want to sit back and enjoy doing nothing. Their do-nothing attitude will qualify them for nothing but the outer darkness. Those who enjoy doing nothing now will be given nothing to do throughout eternity. In contrast, those who enjoy serving now, even though it be as slaves, will be able to enjoy serving then as rulers.

[7] The faith being referenced in 2Pet 1:5 is most readily understood to be the saving faith that results in the regeneration that Peter has just described in the previous verse (2Pet 1:4). Saving faith results in regeneration; saving faith does not necessarily, inevitably, or automatically result in good works. Peter instructs us to add *virtue* (*moral excellence*) to our *faith* (2Pet 1:5). Does this mean that virtue is to be distinguished from our faith? Yes and no. Our virtue has no part in our original faith, but virtue is to be an add-on to our subsequent faith.

[8] Another argument used by those attempting to make works a requirement to reach heaven is to claim that we are not saved by works of the law but by works of faith. Balderdash! Such fiddle-faddle fails to recognize, among other things, that when Paul is refuting the Jewish means of merit in Romans and Galatians, it is understandable that Paul would specify that a person cannot be saved by *works of the law* since these were the types of works through which those under Jewish influence were seeking justification. But when talking to Gentiles, without focusing on Judaizers (where there is no need for that specification), Paul totally rejects works

from consideration. Granted, although the expression *works of the law* may be limited to Romans and Galatians in the Pauline corpus, the concept is not absent entirely elsewhere in his writings. For example, *false circumcision* in Phil 3:2 and *righteousness derived from the law* in Phil 3:9, likewise, would refer to the same type of legalistic moral performance. Still, in excluding works as the means to justification, Paul does not limit comprehensively such works conceptually to works of the law. The rejection of *works* is used more generically in several passages: Eph 2:8-9; 2Tim 1:9, and Tit 3:5. Moral performance of any kind, not just legal obedience performed in obedience to the law, is rejected as a means of reaching heaven.

Moreover, even in the epistle of Romans, Paul bases condemnation on more than just the Jewish works of the law written on paper. Paul also bases condemnation on failure to keep the internal law written in one's heart (Rom 2:15). Paul concludes "that both Jews and Greeks are all under sin" (Rom 3:9). So a few verses later, when Paul goes on to say that we are justified by faith apart from works of the Law (Rom 3:28), he is to be understood as denouncing justification by Jewish or Gentile works stemming from either external or internal law keeping. All works are denounced as a means of justification (in a justification that is by faith apart from works). Additionally, the principle exemplified by Abraham in Rom 4:5-6 (which excludes soteriological justification by works) temporally predates the giving of the external law. Also, the affirmation of *no longer* in Rom 11:6 logically postdates the giving of the Christian law. In conclusion, we are not justified from eternal damnation by Jewish, Gentile, or Christian works.

[9] One well-known costly-free pastor teaches that since the giver gets the glory, believers should never be the givers to God. Otherwise, they would receive the glory. In this costly-free pastor's estimation, God alone is perceived as the Giver and thus the sole recipient of glory. Believers should always be on the receiving end of what is given so that God may get all the glory. After all, as noted by that teacher, God is not "served by human hands, as though He needed anything, since He Himself gives to all life and breath and all things" (Acts 17:25). God does not need our service. We are to serve through the "the strength which God supplies" (1Pet 4:11). God gives us the strength to serve, so the glory belongs to God for our service.

Such a rationale is perforated with errors and only serves (unwittingly perhaps) for a theology that seeks to rob God of His glory in saving us by smuggling in our works as a necessary means for reaching heaven's glory. A Satanic cover-up is discernable in such teaching.

In response to such false teaching, note that God will glorify faithful believers and expects them to seek to be gloried by Him. Believers should love the glory *that comes from God*—to themselves—as a result of their confessing Jesus (Jn 12:42-43; ESV). Christians should be motivated to serve God so that they may hear Him glorify them with the words, "Well done." Christ wants believers to desire to sit on His throne with Him and share His glory. Christ wants believers to want to be co-glorified with Him (Rom 8:17b). God is going to praise faithful believers (1Cor 4:5). Moreover, the Lord is going to cause those who persecute faithful believers to come and bow down at the feet of the persecuted believers (Rev 3:9). Is it wrong for believers to want this—to want what God wants for them? Is God encouraging sinful desires? Surely not! Let not the pseudo pious be allowed to defame God with their silver tongues by attributing godly desires to sin. God wants believers to be motivated by the crown of glory. Seeking glory from God is not shameful. Is desiring to hear, "well done," from earthly fathers a sinful ambition? No. Neither is a desire to hear, "well done," from our Heavenly Father. Not seeking glory from God is sinful. Unwittingly, those pastors who discourage believers from seeking glory are encouraging sin. Moreover, by regarding the believer's desire to receive godly glory as sinful, such pastors are making God the author of sin, since He is the one who encourages such desires in the first place.

Second, although God may not need our service, He certainly wants it. In money management, people are taught to distinguish a *need* from a *want*. Before making a purchase, they are to ask themselves, "Is this a *need* or a *want*?" This costly-free speaker who implied that we should not serve God apparently assumes that since God does not need our service, we are not to give it to Him! To the contrary, even though we are not to serve God as if He needs our service (for His survival), we are to serve God because He desires it (and because He has decided to make the carrying out of many of His plans dependent on our performance). Cannot God willingly make the successful implementation of some of His plans dependent upon our service without needing to do so? Can He not do so out of desire rather than necessity?

Third, this costly-free speaker stressed the fact that God supplies the strength for our service to the exclusion of acknowledging the fact that we provide the service. Certainly, we are to serve God out of the strength which He supplies. Nevertheless, we are the ones who perform the service. God gives the strength, but we give the service. God provides the energy; we supply the effort.

In the follow-up discussion by the class (to which the costly-free speaker's materials were presented), the most tragic statement was a comment made by one of the attendees to the effect that we need to be certain that we depend on God's enablement to perform good works since we cannot be saved by good works. Such a statement seems harmless enough. Actually, it betrays a mentality that is quite deadly.

A prevalent opinion held by many in our pulpits and pews is that one needs God-enabled good works in order to reach heaven. Such people unfortunately think that as long as they trust in God to perform these good works, they can still regard these works as necessary to reach heaven—

without being accused of trusting in their good works as necessary to get to heaven. Not by a long shot!

God provides the enablement, but the works are still our own. Those trusting in God-enabled works to get to heaven are still trusting in their works to get to heaven. Performance-based conditionalism is not going to be able to camouflage its works-righteousness by attributing its service and good works to God's enabling grace, not even if conditionalism attempts to attribute its performance exclusively to God's grace. This satanic cover-up will be unmasked for what it is before God's judgment. God-enabled works are still works—our works! Mistaking or confusing God's enabling grace with His saving grace can have tragic repercussions and produce hellish third-degree burns.

The purpose of judgment is to judge our works (produced through God's enabling grace), not to judge God's independent works (i.e., works done independently of our cooperation and performance). Is God going to judge His own works as lacking? No. However, our works may be lacking.

[10] Some would make an artificial distinction between *help* and *helper* so as to suggest that God helps us but cannot rightly be called our *Helper*. The Scripture, however, while frequently describing God as helping us, does not object to describing God as our Helper: "Thou hast been the helper of the orphan" (Ps 10:14). "O Lord, be my helper" (Ps 30:10). "God is my helper" (Ps 54:4). "The Lord is my helper" (Heb 13:6). Jesus calls the Holy Spirit "another Helper" like Himself (Jn 14:16) and repeatedly refers to the Spirit as our Helper (Jn 14:26; 15:26; 16:27). We are not passive puppets being moved by God's sovereign strings. Benjamin Franklin was correct to conclude in his *Poor Richard's Almanac* that in many aspects: "God helps those who help themselves."

Sometimes it is true that God also helps the helpless (Is 25:4) who cannot help themselves. Salvation from eternal damnation falls into this category. God does all the work. In many cases, however, God helps us by enabling us to help ourselves. For example, if we want God to help us find a job, we cannot expect Him to fill out the job application for us. We are expected to put feet to our prayers and a hand to the pen, not to expect Him to do everything for us. Perseverance falls into this category. By confusing these categories and by making perseverance necessary for final salvation from eternal damnation, costly-free advocates unthinkingly wind up teaching: "God saves those who save themselves."

The Psalmist says of God, "You are my helper and my deliverer!" (Ps 40:17; NET). *Deliverer* is also translatable as *Defender* and *Savior*. Sometimes Christians are enjoined to be "ready to make a defense" (1Pet 3:15). Developing one's skills in Christian apologetics requires work. Not working at being ready to make a defense and expecting God to do all of our work for us would be wrong. Likewise, sometimes the Bible enjoins God's people to save themselves (Jer 48:6; 51:45). Salvation in the present and in the future, indeed, can involve our effort when dealing with rewards. The problem is that by importing perseverance into what is necessary for salvation from hell, conditionalists are making this type of salvation a God-saves-those-who-save-themselves salvation. Logically, in conditionalism, God is no longer pictured as saving a drowning man but a swimming man. If you swim to God's boat, He will pull you in and save you. But you have to swim (persevere) until you reach that boat.

A better picture of what is entailed in salvation from hell is provided by the occasion when Peter, beginning to sink in the sea, "cried out, saying, 'Lord, save me!' And immediately Jesus stretched out His hand and took hold of him, and said to him, 'O you of little faith, why did you doubt?' And when they got into the boat, the wind stopped'" (Mt 14:30-32). Peter was not saved by swimming to the boat or by his grip on his faith or by his grip on Jesus but by Jesus' grip on him. That grip took him all the way to the boat. This physical grip is reminiscent of Jesus' saving grip: "I give eternal life to them, and they shall never perish; and no one shall snatch them out of My hand" (Jn 10:28). When it comes to getting into the boat that takes us to heaven, Jesus does not save those who save themselves but those who call upon Him to save them because they realize that they are helpless to save themselves.

[11] *Believe* is an aorist participle in Lk 8:12. In conjunction with the context, a singular response of faith is seen to result in germination (representing regeneration). Regeneration does not await a protracted period of believing.

[12] Mk 4:19 also uses *ginomai*. Most translations provide some form of *becomes* unfruitful for the thorny soil in these two verses. Some translations render it as some equivalent of *is* unfruitful. A couple of translations translate it as *proves* unfruitful (ESV, RSV). This latter rendition could claim support from BDAG. Although the overall point being made herein does not require that the thorny soil be perceived as bringing forth immature fruit, the parallel from Luke suffices to support the contention that the plant brought forth immature, as opposed to, mature fruit. The implied contrast is between immature fruit and mature fruit. Additionally, both the ESV and RSV correctly pick up on this fact in Lk 8:14, where they both provide the same excellent translation: *their fruit does not mature*. The Greek word for mature in this verse is *telesphoreo* (*telos* + *phero*). Perhaps an eschatological telology is hinted at by this temporal maturity. In any event, lest the proveitist group try to make more out of the *proves unfaithful* translation than what is there, note that BDAG provides this fuller definition for this type of usage: *to come into a certain state or possess certain characteristics, to be, prove to be, turn out to be*. To *turn out to be unfruitful* or to *come into a state of being unfruitful* could turn out to prove more than what the proveitist expositors would want if pressed too far. Are we to think that the plant produced fruit and then became unfruitful? Rather than make such an

argument, the present book is content to embrace the explanation provided by Luke as translated by ESV and RSV. The plant produced fruit, but its fruit did not reach the stage of maturity.

[13] Concerning Mt 13:22, GNTC states that those represented by the third soil persevere in faith. Although this interpretation has not been implemented in the rebuttal of the proveitist position made within the body of the present book, this GES commentator is correct. Because the stated problem *they believe for a while* is affirmed explicitly regarding the second soil (Lk 18:4) and since the parabolic progression implicitly limits the stated problem for each soil type to the one soil type for which it is stated, it stands to reason that the problem of temporary faith is limited to the second soil type. By the same token, the positive affirmation of perseverance in the case of the fourth soil prevents one from affirming that the third soil had the same perseverance being extolled as the forth soil. Thus, the third soil persevered in faith (in contrast to the second soil) but not in faithfulness (in contrast to the fourth soil).

Illustration 75. Positive Progression

❶ Hard	❷ Rocky	❸ Thorny	❹ Good
No Faith	Temporary Faith	Persevering Faith	Persevering Faithfulness

Perseverance in faith is not enough to make it to proveitist heaven. Perseverance in both faith and faithfulness is proveitistically necessary. Not only does this assessment accord well with the details of the parable, proveitists themselves readily acknowledge that within their theology perseverance in faith without corresponding perseverance in good works (i.e., fruits) does not save from hell. In their system of thought, faith without works is soteriologically dead (Jam 2:14-16). They are mistaken within that Jacobean context. In actuality, faith without works is misthologically dead. The same is true in the context of the parable of the soils.

All three of the latter soils believe the same gospel and thus experience genuine faith. The latter two soils persevere in the faith and produce corresponding fruit. Only the fourth soil, however, produces the quality of perseverance necessary for mature fruit. Therefore, within proveitism one cannot point to mere perseverance and fruitfulness as sufficient means of soteriological assurance. Proveitists must be able to discern a sufficiently high qualitative degree of perseverance in fruit production to be reasonably assured of salvation. Within their system, perseverance in faith and in fruit production are not sufficient for assurance of salvation. One must have perseverance in both faith and in **mature** fruit production to qualify for any reasonable level of proveitistic assurance.

[14] This technique is also useful for considering what are thought to be benign proveitist proof texts such as Phil 1:6; 2:15; 1Pet 1:5; 1Jn 2:19. When the proveitist insists that Phil 1:6 means that God will not allow anything to stand in the way of the believer's progressive sanctification, or that Phil 2:15 means that genuine believers will prove themselves as such by the way they live, or that 1Jn 2:19 proves that apostates never were saved in the beginning, or that 1Pet 1:5 guarantees that God will protect the genuine believer from hell by causing that believer to persevere in faith, simply ask, "Why?"

(1) Why is it that God will not allow anything, including the believer's free will, to stand in the way of the believer's practical sanctification? Is it not because proveitists have another group of texts which they believe makes such sanctification necessary to reach heaven (e.g. Phil 3:7-14), so God cannot allow anything to interfere with the progressive sanctification on the part of believers since He has conditioned their glorification on their progression and has assured their glorification? Hence, the proveitist God must assure their progression. (2) Even if *ginomai* were translated as *prove to be* in Phil 2:15, why is this proof necessary? Why do you have to do all things without grumbling (Phil 2:14) in order to prove yourself to be a child of God? What is the outcome of not proving successfully that you are a child of God? Hell? Why? Is it because the proof is judicially necessary in the proveitist courtroom before the proveitist Jesus? Is the outcome conditioned on the proof? If not, why is it important to proveitists to prove that they are children of God in this passage? Is it not to *work out* (in the sense of *securing* and *attaining*) their salvation from the proveitist hell (Phil 2:12)? (3) Why is it that apostasy proves that an apostate never was saved? Is it because in proveitism having eternal life is conditioned on ongoing confession of the Son and obediently abiding in His word so that one will not be cast away into hell in shame at His coming (1Jn 2:23-28)? (4) Why does God need to protect you from hell by causing you to persevere in faith (1Pet 1:5) if perseverance in faith is not necessary for salvation from proveitist hell? And if perseverance is necessary, then why is it not a condition?

Proveitist proof texts and premises lead to the inescapable conclusion that perseverance and good fruits are not only a proveitist necessity to escape hell but are a proveitist condition for salvation from hell. When the logical implications of such supposedly benign proof texts are traced out, the malignant nature of proveitist work-righteousness clearly is seen. For this reason, securitists are readily inclined to provide alternative interpretations for such passages: interpretations that not only avoid conditioning salvation from hell on one's performance but that are also much more in harmony with the contexts of such passages.

[15] As stated within the body of the text: "Many within professing Christendom *genuinely **believe that they believe*** that eternal life is a free

gift. Regrettably, nevertheless, they do not *genuinely* **believe** that eternal life is a free gift—they just believe that they do." The question may be posed in contention: "How can they genuinely believe something they do not genuinely believe?" Actually, such a question misrepresents the situation. Rather, proveitists genuinely believe that they believe something they do not genuinely believe. Clarification centers around observing the double proposition.

To believe is to be persuaded that a proposition is true. To believe that 2 + 2 = 4 is to accept that statement as true. What if someone genuinely believes a mistaken proposition though, such as 2 + 2 = 5? Such faith would be genuine yet mistaken. The statement *proveitists* **believe** *that they* **believe** *that eternal life is free* poses two distinct propositions as noted by the double occurrence of both the verb *believe* and the pronoun *that*:

- They **believe** (1) *that* they **believe** (2) *that* eternal life is free.

Proveitists genuinely (yet mistakenly) **believe** *that they* **believe** *that eternal life is free*. The first proposition is genuinely believed. The second proposition is not genuinely believed. Proveitists do not genuinely *believe that eternal life is a free gift*. Nevertheless, they genuinely *believe that they believe that eternal life is free*.

Illustration 76. I Believe that I Believe

The kernel of saving faith is found in the second proposition. Proveitists do not believe it. Nevertheless, they genuinely believe that they believe it. Logically, though, they certainly do not. They are prevented from believing that eternal life is genuinely free by actually believing that they must live better to get to heaven.

Although I was a math major in college, when I was helping my sons with their junior high school math homework, I was still very appreciative of the answers in the back of book for the odd problems, especially when we were doing the word problems. All of us have probably struggled with mathematical word problems at one time or another. Those problems can be particularly tough. You can work through the problem and think that you understand how to work it. But when you look in the back of the book, you may find that the answer that you believe that you have correctly derived is wrong. Or alas, you might even occasionally look in the back of the math book and mistakenly look up the wrong answer.

Like looking in the back of the math book for the answer to the odd problems, some people have looked at the answer verses in the Bible, which clearly state that eternal life is a free gift, and have assumed that they understand how to work the problem verses that state that eternal life is a reward. They think that they have figured out how to work the word problem by concluding that eternal life is a free gift that they receive as a free reward for the way they live. Logically, this answer is nonsense. Tragically, they have mismatched the equation and answer. Like someone mistakenly looking up the right answer to the wrong question in the back of the math book, they have taken a verse from one context and made it the answer for a verse in a different context to produce a result that was never intended by the author of the book. Whether it is word problems in the Bible pertaining to eternal life or math problems in junior high school, they cannot blame the Bible or the math book when they apply the wrong answer to the wrong word problem.

Illustration 77. Mathematical Problems and Answers

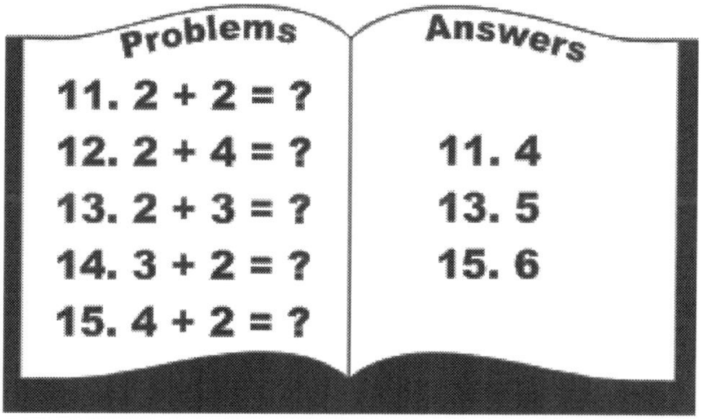

Problems	Answers
11. 2 + 2 = ?	11. 4
12. 2 + 4 = ?	
13. 2 + 3 = ?	13. 5
14. 3 + 2 = ?	15. 6
15. 4 + 2 = ?	

To simplify the illustration, simple arithmetic is used in the above math book. Suppose a child working on problem 11 mistakenly looks in the back of the book at the answer for problem 13. The child would conclude that 2 + 2 = 5, genuinely believing that this is the correct answer for 2 + 2. The problem is not that the child does not believe in the numerical value of 4 but that the child does not believe that 4 is the result of 2 + 2. In math, as well as in Scripture, matching the right answer with the right equation is necessary.

Illustration 78. Soteriological Problems and Answers

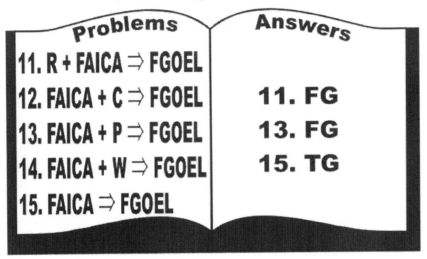

- R = Repentance from bad behavior
- C = Commitment to perform better
- P = Perseverance
- FAICA = Faith alone in Christ alone
- FGOEL = Free gift of eternal life
- FG = False gospel
- TG = True gospel

Similarly, using a soteriological book to represent the biblical problem, most people wrongly consider at least one of the expressions in 11-14 to be true. They believe that FGOEL is the result of some type (or multiple types) of performance. Consequently, they do not believe that FGOEL is the result of FAICA. That is, they do not believe that the *free gift of eternal life* is the result of *faith alone in Christ alone*. Nevertheless, they believe in the concept of the FGOEL (*free gift of eternal life*). It is as if they are saying, "I believe in the *free gift of eternal life*, except I just don't believe that it is free." The addition of such an exception nullifies their confession. God requires that the perception of eternal life as a free gift be derived from the proper equation. Otherwise, saving faith has not genuinely occurred.

Theoretically, proveitists believe in the possibility of the FGOEL. At least in theory, FGOEL might exist on the proveitistic chalkboard. Moreover, when proveitists are speaking at the theoretically level, it sounds like they really believe that eternal life is a free gift. Practically speaking, however, proveitists do not believe that the possession of eternal life as a free gift actually exists independent of one's performance.

[16] In Mt 7:13-14, the hard part is finding the gate, not following the path to life. The question is, "Can you find the path?" The costly-free speaker mistakenly thought that the issue was, "Can you stay on the path?" It is hard to believe that one can be saved merely by believing in Jesus for eternal life. It is much easier to believe that entrance into heaven is attained by performance. The costly-free speaker unwittingly was taking the easy way out and thus missing out on what Jesus was saying.

[17] Proveitists cannot condition salvation on faith apart from works since they condition salvation on perseverance, which is itself a work. They cannot affirm salvation from hell by faith apart from works since they affirm salvation by works as the necessary evidence of faith. Justification independent of works is impossible in a theology that makes justification dependent upon works. One cannot be saved apart from works by a proveitist faith that needs works to be saving. A justification that is given because of works cannot be equated with a justification that is given apart from works.

[18] Proveitists who seek to overstate the distinction between *basis/by* and *according to* claim that the verdict is *according to works* but the *ground* or *basis* for acquittal is really Christ's righteousness, not our own. According to this proveitist claim, salvation from hell merely is *according to* works, not *based on* works or *by* works. This thoroughgoing distinction will not bear up under scrutiny and represents a futile attempt on their part to disassociate themselves with teaching works-righteousness.

Negatively, according to Paul, salvation from hell is not on the *basis of* (*ek*) our works (Tit 3:5) or *according to* (*kata*) our works (2Tim 1:9). The exclusion of *ek* works is used synonymously for an exclusion of *kata* works. Similarly, Christ was not made our Priest on *the basis* (*kata*) of a physical law (Heb 7:6). Will we imagine that Christ was made our Priest *according to* a physical law? Of course not! Positively, both *ek* and *kata* may be used synonymously and translated interchangeably as *basis* or *according to* (Rev 20:12). The affirmation of *ek* works is used as a confirmation of *kata* works.

Contrastively, righteousness *by* (*ek*) faith is juxtaposed with righteousness *by* (*ek*) works (Rom 9:32). The purpose of this contrast is not to suggest that this type of righteousness is *kata* works. The denial of *ek* works implies a denial of *kata* works—for the type of righteousness that is given as a gift resulting in heavenly entrance.

On the other hand, the type of righteousness that results in a reward can be *according to (kata)* faith (Heb 11:7). This verse is talking about the type of faith necessary to obtain the reward of the inheritance (cp. Heb 11:6). Being declared righteous in this sense would be a reward. Indeed, this whole chapter (in Heb 11) is saturated with the dative expression *by faith* and describes what people did by faith in order to obtain heavenly rewards (cp. Heb 11:26). They are rewarded by God because of their virtuous faith. Whether that faith is expressed in Greek by the dative or accusative case is immaterial: "*By faith* [dative] Noah, being warned by God about things not yet seen, in reverence prepared an ark for the salvation of his household, by which he condemned the world, and became an heir of the righteousness which is *according to faith* [accusative]" (Heb 11:7). Rewards are *according to* works, earned *by works*. In this context, faith is a work since it results in a reward. Since persevering faith may result in reward, heaven cannot be the result of persevering faith because heaven is not a reward.

[19] Also, the Bible clearly affirms a justification *by (ek)* works (Jam 2:21,24-25) in addition to a justification *by (ek)* faith (Rom 5:1; Gal 3:24). Works bear the same semantic relationship to the *bema* justification described by James as faith does to the justification from hell described by Paul. Just as the justification that saves us from hell is by faith, the justification that saves us from the outer darkness is by works. One justification is by faith; the other justification is by works. Insisting that judgment is always *according to works* rather than *based on (by)* works deals artificially with justification by works. Justification *by works* before God at His *bema* is *according to* a judgment *by works*.

Proveitists would acknowledge that initial salvation is not on the *basis of (ek)* works (Rom 11:6; Tit 3:5). Would they thereby insist that this means that initial salvation is *according to* works? No! Paul is not merely denying works as a *basis* for salvation from hell; he also intends for us to understand that initial salvation (i.e., salvation from hell) is not *according to (kata)* works (2Tim 1:9). In denying that works are the *basis* for this type of salvation, Paul is denying that this salvation is *according to* works. The proveitist claim that final salvation (from hell) is *according to* works rather than on the *basis of* works drives a false wedge between the two expressions. A judgment *according to* works would be a judgment *based on* works. Paul asserts that initial salvation is **not** *ek/kata* works. For proveitists to turn around and claim that this salvation, in the end, proves to be salvation *kata* works rather than *ek* works only proves that proveitists have distorted the biblical record.

When Paul says that salvation from hell is not a *result of (ek)* works (Eph 2:8-9), he is not leaving open a loop-hole for proveitists to claim that salvation from hell is *according to (kata)* works. To the contrary, this salvation is *apart from (choris)* works (Rom 3:28; 4:6). Judgment, in contrast, is not apart from works. Judgment is according to works. The

Endnotes

verdict given by judgment is given as a result of works. The verdict is by works.

Purely-free advocates are not claiming that good works produced by believers provide the basis in the sense of providing the grounds for rewards. When speaking of righteousness (or other benefits) that come to believers on the *basis of* faith (*ek* Rom 10:6; *epi* Acts 3:16; Phil 3:9), that faith is understood to be the condition rather than grounds for the blessing. Even so, works provide the condition for the reward. Good works do not cause God to reward us; rather, God rewards us because of our good works. To be judged and rewarded because of one's good works is to be judged and rewarded based on one's good works.

Some may object that judgment is not always based on works since "mercy triumphs over judgment" and mercy is not a work (Jam 2:13). In anticipation of such an objection, note that James is talking about works of mercy. Works of mercy will triumph on judgment day because judgment is always based on works—in this case, works of mercy.

As an aside, note that perseverance in faith is a work. Believers will be judged and rewarded according to whether they persevere in faith. Since rewards always are based on works, and since perseverance in faith is rewarded, perseverance is a work. Therefore, to condition salvation from hell on perseverance in faith is to teach a false gospel that conditions salvation from hell on works. Perseverance in faith is excluded from consideration in a salvation conditioned on faith apart from works since a salvation by faith apart from works cannot be a salvation conditioned on perseverance which is a work.

[20] F. Andersen, *2 Enoch*. Longer recension, manuscript J. Available at http://www.marquette.edu/maqom/slavonicenoch.html. Accessed on December 26, 2009.

Indexes

Italic, regular, and bold fonts have been used for page numbers within the indexes to rank entrees in terms of emphases as: *minor*, medium, **major**.

Greek Index

airo	27
akarpos	66
alogos	4
basileia	27
bebaios	**49**
bema	14, 83
choris	142
doulos	**19**
ek	**122, 141, 142**
ekballo	**31**
emphutos	**57**
epi	*143*
epichoregeo	46, 48
eris	38
eschatos	30
ginomai	66, **92, 93, 135,** 137
gregoreo	*17*
huios	29
karpos	**66**
kata	**122, 141, 142**
krupto	23, 24
kruptos	23
logikos	4
logos	*3, 4*
ouk	*63*
phero	135
phuo	57, 64
pistos	17
plousios	49
poluteles	45
prolego	41
rhiza	*63*
sarkikos	37
speiro	64
spoudazo	49
spoude	**49**
stephanos	45
sumphuo	64
sun	**93**
teknon	29
telesphoreo	**135**
telos	135
theos	*3*
xeraino	**54**
zelos	38

Subject Index

abide 53, 54, **59**
abundant
    entrance **48**, 53
    life 10, 61
accursed 5
accusative 142
addition 48
adjective 57
adverb 57
alert 17
animals 4, 130
aorist participle 135
apart from works
    basic entrance 48
    because of works *141*
    biblical 5
    dependent on works 93
    does not exist 70
    faith that works 81
    God-enabled
works 86
justification by works 83
necessary 51
necessary evidence *141*
needs works 5, *141*
of the Law 132
perseverance *141*, 143
apologetics 134
apostates **137**
assurance 53, **56, 58, 61,** 89, **136**
bad believers 69
barter 5
bath of regeneration 52
beg the question 73
believe
    and be saved 56, **60**
    be persuaded 138
    for a while 59, **60**
    that they believe ... 49, **113, 114, 115, 137**
believers

Indexes

immature 23
mature 23
bema fire 92
benign 137
Benjamin Franklin 134
Book of
   Life 30, **123**
   Works **122**
breathing 106
building the tower **73**
but for the grace of God 86
calling and election 49
carnal **37**
   behavior 13, 64
   believers **38**, 80, 104, **116**
   security
      rudimentary 70
      unmediated **71**
   state 119
cast
   into the fire 92
   out **31**, 131
cause 76
character 8, 45, **46–54**, 53
   development 45, 51
   traits 51
   virtue 45
   worthy of reward 47
charge of
   many things 44
   performance 38
   these cities 119
children 29
Christ-enabled
   performance **85**
church age 14
clean slate 52, 53
co-heirs 110
collective singular *81*
command 53
commitment 2, 40, 80, **111**
   of life 38, 40
condition 54
   necessary requirement 108
   not basis 143
   reap 41
conditionalists
   lose-it 55
   prove-it **55**
confession 92
congruent reward 129
contrapositive 73
control of life 39, **116**
costly **6**
costly-free **6**
count the cost **73**, 83
courtroom **76**, 92
covenantal

relationship 20, 27, 29
cover-up 132, 134
criticism
   of soils 60
crop 67
crown
   of life 8, 10, 42, 45, 109, 110, 117
dative 142
David 36
deceive themselves 114
demonic nature 64
dinner 126
disciples 54, **92**
   fledged 92
   full-fledged 92
   not born 119
   secret 92
   unfledged 92
distributive plurals *81*
do your best **49**
doers of the word 60
dogs 112
downhill ride 102
downstream 39, 51
drowning 135
dying thief 99
effort 52, 133
elect Jews 27
enablement **134**
enabling
   grace **93**
   power 52
energy 52
Enoch **126**
entrance 43
   abundant **48**
   rich 49
entrusted
   believers **20**
entrustment
   types 23
equal opportunity employer 129
equations
   $2 + 2 = 4$ 138
   $2 + 2 = 5$ 138, 140
   FAICA $\Rightarrow$ FGOEL 140
   FAICA + P $\Rightarrow$ FGOEL + C 140
   FAICA + W $\Rightarrow$ FGOEL 140
   free $\leftrightarrow$ costly 117
   R+ FAICA $\Rightarrow$ FGOEL 140
eschatology 30
eternal
   kingdom 49
   life
      duality 9, **100**
      gift 139
      possession 99, 100
      quality **99**

reap 41
reward 139
source **99**
threshold 99
two-dimensional 98
ethnic
    Jews 28
evidence **46**, **75**, 122
    necessary 61
FAICA 140
faith
    and works **46–54**, 48
    apart from works 5
    dead 90
    evidence of **46**
    fiathful 17
    great 98
    initial 47, 53
    is a work 142
    little 98
    needs works 5
    persevering 61
    purity 61
    quality 61
    quantity 61
    saving 61
    temporary 61, **136**
    that works 48, 81
    virtuous 53, 142
    without works 81, 83
faith + works 47
faithfulness 45
faith-works 46, 47
fall
    away **59**
    from grace 104
    out… 59
false convert 62
fellowship 30, 100
FGOEL 140
filling in blank 41
final
    justification 75
    salvation 49, 75, 76, 79
finite 100
fire 32
    bema 92
    hell… 32
fit for the kingdom 74
fizzle out 116
flat tire 89
flesh 64
flowerpot 46
follower 92
foolish virgins 130
foretell 41
forewarn 41
forfeitist 55

forgiveness
    initial 53
    provisional 52
    reward 52
    salvific 53
former sins **52**
free will *137*
friends
    legalistic 118
    licentious 117
fruit **39**
    active **50**
    as necessary proof **35**
    because we are saved 39
    condition 79, **137**
    degree 92
    effort 50
    immature **66**
    mature **56**
    necessary 78, **137**
        evidence 79
    not passive 54, 66
    of Spirit **35**, **36**, 45, 68, 81
    passive 97
    praiseworthy 68
    proves 56
    purity 97
    quality 78, 81, 97
    quantitative 92
    quantity 81
    regeneration 40
    runty 56
    saving faith 88
    singular **81**
    to be saved 39
    wholly good 82
fruits **27**
    plural 83
gates
    hell… **127**
    paradise **127**
germination 55, 60, 135
giving
    God the glory 51
    to God 132
glorification 137
glory **132**
God
    dependent 133
    desire 133
    Helper 52
    need **133**
    the glory 51
    will not keep 77
God-enabled 49, **69**, **133**
    fruit 83
    grace 49, **87**
    legalism 83

Indexes

performance 71, **86**, 88, 89, 108
righteousness 83, 85
works 129, **133**
godly performance 89
good
    fight 8
    neighbor 93
    works
        God-enabled 133
Great Tribulation 16
Great White Throne Judgment **122**
grew up 57
grounds 122
guarantee 49
hacksaw 71
hamster 117
hand to the plow 74
heirs of God 110
Helper **134**
helpless 134
hidden costs 62
honest and good **67**
hypothetical 75
image of God 3
immature 119
immune to gospel 112
imperishable 58, 59
implanted **57**
impossible
    logically 3
impressible seed 70
infant stage 119
infinite 100
inherit the kingdom **38**, **42**
inheritance 27, 40, **42**, 45, 94
irrationalism 116
It is finished **113**
jealousy 38
Jesus
    infinite 100
Jews 27, 29
    unworthy stewards 22
Joseph of Arimathea 23, 24
joy of salvation 36
Judaizers 131
judgment 11
    according to works 121
    bema 58
    by works 122
    for works **121**
    merciless **90**
    on basis of works 122
    seat 26
justification
    by faith **85**, 142
    by works 83, 142
    declarative 88
    manifestative 75, 88

kingship 27, 94, **105**
Lake of Fire 106
lamp 23
laugh in Jesus' face 104
law of non-contradiction 3, 8
legalism 13
    definition 129
    God-enabled 129
    hard **95**
    soft **95**
let go let God 50
licentiousness **12**
light **24**, 25
live like the devil 13, *129*
logic **3**
looking back 74
Lord
    of all 116
    of your life 116
lose eternal life
    Jesus **99**
    quantitatively 100
loss of rewards 103
Lucifer 129
lying 6
malignant 137
manifestation 86
    necessary 75
manifestative righteousness 88, **89**
math problems 139
mathematical certainty 19
maturity
    eschatology 135
    temporal 135
merciless judgment 83
mercy **91**
    costly-free **95**
    earned **94**
    unearned **94**
merit 50, 68, 97
    inherent **45**, 46
    inherit 45
natural 38
necessary 76
negation
    relative 63
new
    nature **23**, 64
non-things 99
old nature 64
Once Saved Always Saved 9
OSAS 9, 61
out of the closet 92
outer darkness 117, 119
    cast out **31**
    eternal 118
    exclusion 44
    for entrusted **20**

for hiding new nature 23
for identical relationships 27
for non-alert 17
for own 19
for those who received 29
suffer loss 30
term 32
time of judgment 25
timing 30
unknown time of return 19
warning to believers 18
weep and gnash teeth 32
paddle
hearts out 42
upstream 40, **42**, 44
palace 125
parable
of the laborers 129
of the sower 55
of the steward 23
of the talents **16**
paradise 125
pay the price 129
perseverance 137, 142, 143
conditional 107
in faith 136
in faithfulness 136
necessary **106**
quality 136
Pharisee 85, 87, 96
modern day **88**
pie in the sky **91**, 104
practical sanctification 35
practice 48
precious 45
primary application 22, 23
prize 102
prodigal
son **28**
Promised Land 100
proof
judicial 137
prophetic
foreshortening 16, 19
year 16
prove to be 137
proveitists 73
proves 135
psychological
association 112
psychologists 112
publican **87**, 95
puppets 93
purely free **9**
quench the Spirit 64
rapture 14, 16
rational 4
reap 41, 45

eternal life **41**
regeneration 22, 73, 106
not talent **25**
relationship 30, 100
relative
negation 63
relatively good 88
remain 54
repentance 2
revelation
progressive 26
revolving door salvation 116
rewards
negative **11**
positive **11**
works 11
righteousness
for entrance 142
for inheritance 142
imparted 5
imputed 5
root
deep 63
determines
destiny **75**
fruit **35**, 42, 55, 63, **75**
false 64
true 64
firm 63
fruit canoe **39**
immature 63
mature **65**
none **62**, 63
of regeneration 51
rowing 39
running 117
salvation 40
final 5, 40
of soul 57, 58, 71
of spirit 58
revolving door 116
save themselves 134
validation 93
sanctification 137
progressive 119
regressive 119
save soul 58
saved
by fruit 39
by root 39
saving
faith 81
kernal 139
quality 97
singular 97
grace **93**
secondary
application 23

secure	**49**
securitist	55
Securitist	
keep-it	55
seed	62, 69
of life	71
self	
on the throne	116
seven years	16
shallow converts	62
Sheep and Goats	121
shock	112
shorten	
the number of days	19
should	24
sins	100
slave	**19**
soil	
determines the fruit	55
good	66, **67**
hard	**56**
rocky	**57**
thorny	**64**, 66
Son of God	100
sons	28
ethnic	28
of the kingdom	**28**, 62
soul	
loss of	30
sovereignty	61
sow to the Spirit	41
sower	62, 69
spiritual	4, 38
gifts	23, **130**
maturity	119
sprouts	60
stewardship	30
strife	38
subconscious	111
suffer loss	**30**
sweat	
God	50
ours	52
swimming	135
taken away	27
talent	**22, 25**, 130
talk to the animals	130
tares	**62**
telology	*135*
temporary faith	56, 61, **136**
the way you live	40
thorns	64

three types of people	116
threshold	99
throne of life	**116**
time of return	14
tombstones	115
tone	112
tongues	130
train dogs	112
tribulation	14
unconditional security	9
unconsciously poisoned	111
unfruitful	66, 135
uphill fight	**101**
ups and downs	99
upstream	39, 51
vice list	**35**
victor's crown	45
vineyard	129
virtue	45
virtuous	
faith	**46**
woman	45
walk by Spirit	41
want	**133**
warn	
Christians	40
water of life	8
weeping	**32**
wither	**54**
without	
cost	**5**
money	5
word problems	139
works	
according to	**142**
added to faith	46
attributed to God	51
basis	**142**
burned up	54
derived from faith	47
grounds	95
mere evidence	48
necessary	95
of faith	131
of the law	**131**, 132
works-righteousness	**5, 111, 112**
worse than an unbeliever	**89**
worthless believers	31
worthy	125
Zaccheus	22
zero virtue	48

Extrabiblical Index

2En 42:1-5 ... **127**	2En 42:5 ... **125**

Scripture Index

Reference	Page
Ruth 2:12	*121*
1Sam 26:23	*121*
2Sam 3:39	*121*
2Sam 22:5	*121*
2Sam 22:21	*121*
2Chron 15:7	*121*
Job 34:11	*121*
Job 38:7	131
Job 41:11	*121*
Ps 10:14	*134*
Ps 18:20	*121*
Ps 18:24	*121*
Ps 28:4	*121*
Ps 30:10	*134*
Ps 40:17	*134*
Ps 51:12	36
Ps 54:4	*134*
Ps 62:11	*121*
Ps 62:12	*121*
Prov 24:12	*121*
Prov 31:10	45
Is 1:18	4
Is 5:20	3
Is 25:4	134
Is 40:10	121
Is 55:1	5
Is 55:6-7	4
Is 55:8-9	4
Is 59:18	*121*
Is 62:11	*121*
Is 64:6	83
Jer 17:10	*121*
Jer 25:14	*121*
Jer 31:16	*121*
Jer 32:19	*121*
Jer 48:6	*134*
Jer 50:29	*121*
Jer 51:24	*121*
Jer 51:45	*134*
Lam 3:64	*121*
Eze 7:9	*121*
Eze 24:14	*121*
Eze 36:19	*121*
Dan 9:24-27	16
Hos 4:9	*121*
Hos 12:2	*121*
Zech 14:4	16
Mt 5:7	**91**
Mt 5:13	31
Mt 5:14-16	24
Mt 5:15-16	23
Mt 5:19	83
Mt 5:22	*32*
Mt 6:4	*121*
Mt 6:18	*121*
Mt 7:13-14	115, 141
Mt 7:15-20	77
Mt 7:19	75, **78**, 81
Mt 7:23	83
Mt 8:10	98
Mt 8:12	**28**, 31, *32*, 62, 98
Mt 10:22	103
Mt 10:33	103
Mt 13:6	54, 63
Mt 13:8	66
Mt 13:18	55
Mt 13:21	**63**
Mt 13:22	66, **136**
Mt 13:27	*19*
Mt 13:38	62
Mt 13:40	*32*
Mt 13:42	*32*
Mt 13:47-50	28
Mt 13:50	*32*
Mt 14:30-32	135
Mt 16:24-27	30
Mt 16:27	*121*
Mt 18:8-9	*32*
Mt 20:1-16	129
Mt 21:28-32	29
Mt 21:43	**21, 27**
Mt 22:11-13	**32**, 125
Mt 22:13	31, *32*
Mt 22:14	125
Mt 24:3	18
Mt 24:3-4	*18*
Mt 24:9-14	16
Mt 24:13	103
Mt 24:22	16, 19
Mt 24:42	15
Mt 24:42-43	**18**
Mt 24:44	15
Mt 24:45	23
Mt 24:51	*32*
Mt 25:13	*18*, 19, 26
Mt 25:14	19, 20
Mt 25:14-30	**14**, 17
Mt 25:15	20
Mt 25:18	23
Mt 25:19	14, 25
Mt 25:20	27
Mt 25:21	27, *30*, 44
Mt 25:23	27, *30*
Mt 25:24	92
Mt 25:25	*17*
Mt 25:26	27, 90
Mt 25:27	26, 30
Mt 25:28	30
Mt 25:28-29	27
Mt 25:30	30, 31, *32*
Mt 25:34-35	121
Mt 25:41	*32*

Indexes

Mk 4:6	63
Mk 4:17	63
Mk 4:19	135
Mk 13:3	18
Mk 13:3-5	18
Mk 13:20	19
Mk 15:34	**99**
Lk 3:9	*75*
Lk 8:4-15	**55**
Lk 8:5	56
Lk 8:6	**57, 59**
Lk 8:7	64
Lk 8:8	66
Lk 8:12	**56**, 59, **60**, 74, 135
Lk 8:13	**59**, 63, 75
Lk 8:14	64, 66, 135
Lk 8:15	54, 67
Lk 9:23	6
Lk 9:62	74, 105
Lk 10:36	93
Lk 11:33	23
Lk 13:7	*75*
Lk 13:9	*75*
Lk 13:28	31
Lk 14:14	*121*
Lk 14:26-27	92
Lk 14:26-33	6
Lk 14:28	**73**
Lk 14:33	92
Lk 17:30	*16*
Lk 18:4	**136**
Lk 18:9-14	**85**
Lk 19:17-19	119
Lk 19:21	*17*
Lk 19:24-26	21
Lk 22:44	99
Lk 23:43	99
Jn 1:12	59
Jn 2:23-24	*23*
Jn 2:24	21, **22, 23**
Jn 4:10	5
Jn 5:24	11, 124
Jn 6:37	**31**, 131
Jn 6:47	60, 115
Jn 6:60-65	92
Jn 8:31	92
Jn 10:3-4	19
Jn 10:10	10
Jn 10:14	19
Jn 10:28	*99*, 135
Jn 12:42-43	*23*, 92, 132
Jn 14:6	3, *99*
Jn 14:16	*134*
Jn 14:26	*134*
Jn 15:4-8	**53**
Jn 15:5	92
Jn 15:6	31, **54**, 74, 92, 103, 131
Jn 15:8	92
Jn 15:10	54
Jn 15:26	*134*
Jn 16:27	*134*
Jn 17:2	*99*
Jn 19:30	113
Jn 19:38	*23*, 92
Acts 3:16	*143*
Acts 11:26	92
Acts 12:22-23	88
Acts 13:46	22
Acts 14:22	105
Acts 17:25	**132**
Rom 2:6	*121*
Rom 2:15	132
Rom 3:2	21
Rom 3:9	132
Rom 3:28	5, 132, *142*
Rom 4:5-6	132
Rom 4:6	5, *142*
Rom 5:1	*142*
Rom 5:15-16	5
Rom 6:23	*99*
Rom 8:12	*100*
Rom 8:13	100, 103
Rom 8:14-17	**110**
Rom 8:17	133
Rom 8:21	131
Rom 10:6	*143*
Rom 10:17	56
Rom 11:6	88, 132
Rom 11:6;	*142*
Rom 11:15	*121*
Rom 12:1	**4**
Rom 14:10-12	12
1Cor 2:14-3:3	**38**
1Cor 3:11-15	23, 26, 30
1Cor 3:14	*121*
1Cor 3:14-15	103
1Cor 3:15	21, 54, 101
1Cor 4:5	133
1Cor 9:17	21
1Cor 9:23-27	102
1Cor 13:8-10	**130**
1Cor 15:2	103
1Cor 15:10	93
2Cor 5:10	12, 121
Gal 1:8-9	5
Gal 2:7	*21*
Gal 3:7	*29*
Gal 3:24	*142*
Gal 3:26	*29*
Gal 5:4	44, 103
Gal 5:16-21	**38, 39**
Gal 5:19-21	**35**
Gal 5:21	**40, 41, 42**, *100*
Gal 5:22	45
Gal 5:22-23	**35**
Gal 5:25	41

Gal 6:7-9	**41**, **42**
Eph 2:8	131
Eph 2:8-9	93, *132*, 142
Eph 2:10	93
Eph 5:5	94
Eph 5:8-9	24
Eph 6:7-8	94
Phil 1:6	**137**
Phil 2:12	137
Phil 2:13	52
Phil 2:14	137
Phil 2:15	**137**
Phil 3:2	132
Phil 3:7-14	*137*
Phil 3:9	132, *143*
Col 1:22-23	103
Col 1:29	52
Col 2:13	52
Col 2:13-14	99
Col 3:23-25	40, **42**
Col 3:24	45
Col 3:25	12
1Thess 2:4	*21*
1Thess 4:17	16
2Thess 1:4-5	105
2Thess 1:7	*16*
2Thess 3:11-15	90
1Tim 1:11	*21*
1Tim 4:16	103
1Tim 5:8	89
1Tim 6:20	*21*
2Tim 1:9	*132*, 142
2Tim 1:14	*21*
2Tim 2:12	10, 103, 105
2Tim 4:7-8	**8**
2Tim 4:14	*121*
Tit 1:3	*21*
Tit 1:9	3
Tit 3:5	5, *52*, *132*, 141, *142*
Heb 3:17-4:1	101
Heb 10:26-27	103
Heb 10:30	*121*
Heb 10:35-26	105
Heb 11:6	102, *142*
Heb 11:7	**142**
Heb 11:26	*142*
Heb 13:6	*134*
Jam 1:12	*8*, *45*, 105
Jam 1:18	**58**
Jam 1:21	**57**, 58
Jam 1:22	92
Jam 2:13	**90**, 143
Jam 2:13-26	90
Jam 2:14-16	136
Jam 2:14-17	**90**
Jam 2:20	83
Jam 2:21	83, 142
Jam 2:24-25	83, 142
Jam 3:10	**64**
Jam 3:10-12	**64**
Jam 3:12	**65**
1Pet 1:5	**137**
1Pet 1:17	*121*
1Pet 1:23	58, **59**
1Pet 2:9	22
1Pet 3:4	45
1Pet 3:15	134
1Pet 4:11	**132**
2Pet 1:4	131
2Pet 1:5	*48*, *49*, 131
2Pet 1:5-11	45, **46–54**
2Pet 1:8	66
2Pet 1:9	**52**
2Pet 1:10	48, **49**
2Pet 1:11	48, 53
2Pet 2:12	*4*
1Jn 2:19	**137**
1Jn 2:23-28	*137*
1Jn 3:17-18	90
2Jn 1:8	21
Jude 1:10	*4*
Rev 2:4	117
Rev 2:5	117
Rev 2:10	*8*, *45*
Rev 2:23	*121*
Rev 3:9	133
Rev 3:11	21, *100*
Rev 8:12	19
Rev 18:6	*121*
Rev 20:12	141
Rev 20:12-13	*121*, 122
Rev 20:12-15	**123**
Rev 22:12	11, *121*
Rev 22:17	5

Made in the USA
Lexington, KY
16 October 2014